FDDI
An Introduction to
Fiber Distributed Data Interface

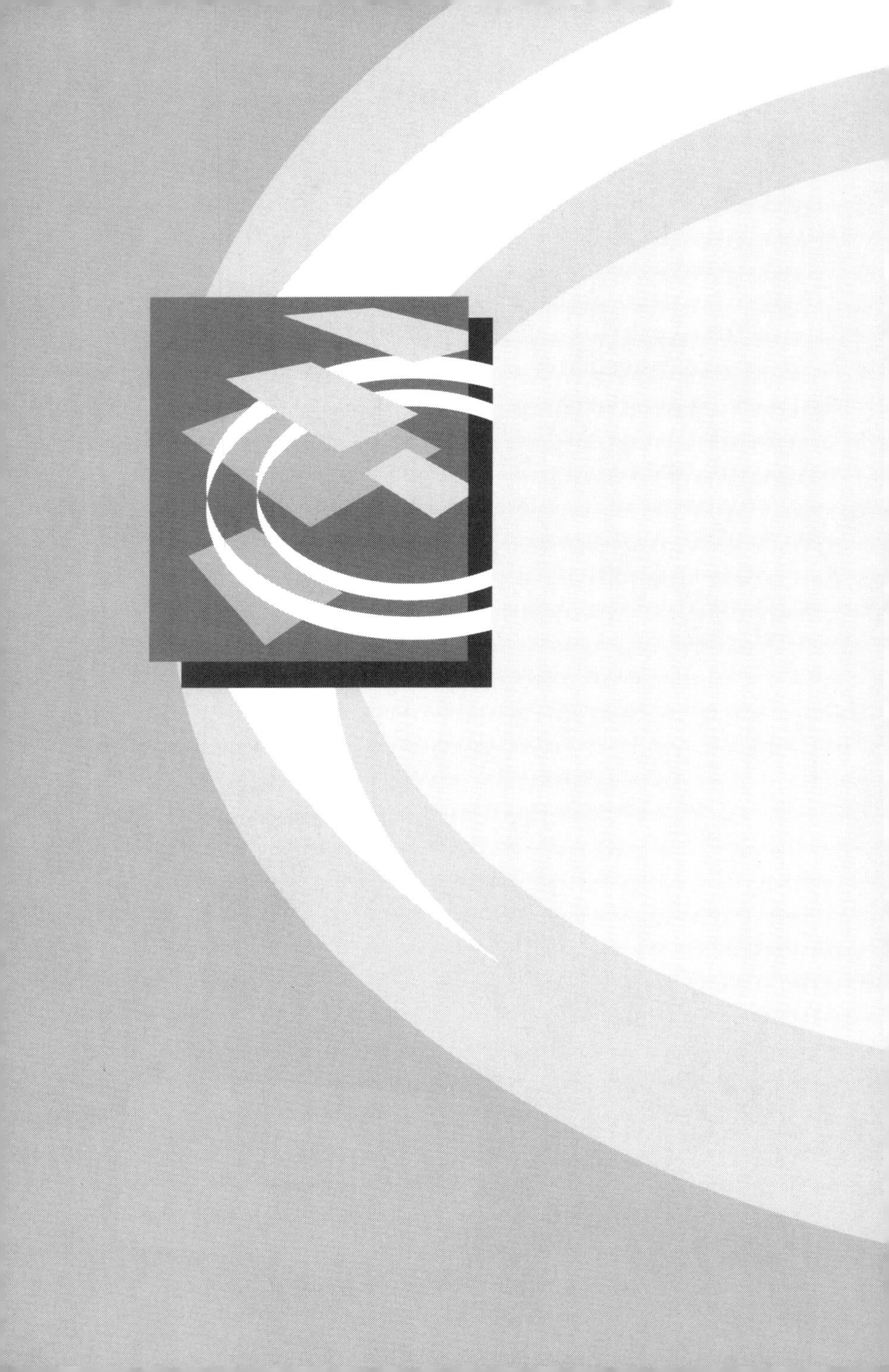

FDDI
An Introduction to
Fiber Distributed Data Interface

Wendy H. Michael
William J. Cronin, Jr.
Karl F. Pieper

digital

Digital Press

Printed in the United States of America

9 8 7 6 5 4 3 2 1

Order number EY-J840E-DP

The publisher offers discounts on bulk orders of this book. For information, please write to:

Special Sales Department
Digital Press
One Burlington Woods Drive
Burlington, MA 01803

The publisher believes the information in this book is accurate as of its publication date; such information is subject to change without notice. Digital Equipment Corporation is not responsible for any errors that may appear in this book.

AppleTalk is a registered trademark of Apple Computer, Inc.
Chipcom is a registered trademark of Chipcom Corporation.
applicationDEC, DEC, DECbridge,DECconcentrator, DECmcc, DECnet, DECstation, Digital, the Digital logo, LAT, ThinWire, TURBOchannel, ULTRIX, VAX, VAXcluster, and VMS are trademarks of Digital Equipment Corporation.
Motorola is a registered trademark of Motorola, Inc.
Novell and NetWare are registered trademarks of Novell, Inc.
SCO is a trademark of Santa Cruz Operations, Inc.
UNIX is a registered trademark of UNIX system laboratories, Inc.

Library of Congress Cataloging-in-Publication Data

Michael, Wendy H.
    FDDI: an introduction to fiber distributed data interface / Wendy
    H. Michael, William J. Cronin, Karl F. Pieper.
        p. cm.
    Includes index.
    ISBN 1-55558-093-9
    1. Local area networks (Computer networks). 2. Fiber Distributed
    Data Interface (Computer network standard). 3. Cronin, William J.
    II. Pieper, Karl F. III. Title.
TK51505.7.M52 1992
004.6'8---dc20   92-27167
                                                      CIP

Contents

Preface

Fiber Distributed Data Interface (FDDI) is a set of standards for local area networks developed under the American National Standards Institute and approved for international use by the International Standards Organization. As a networking standard that has grown out of consensus, FDDI stands in contrast to other local area network systems, which are frequently associated with specific vendors. FDDI is widely accepted and supported in the industry as the next-generation international standard for high-speed, multivendor networking interconnections.

Initially based on the use of fiber optics technology and advanced product design, FDDI networks can transfer increased amounts of data much faster and over longer distances than conventional local area networks. FDDI is a 100-megabit-per-second technology that uses a timed-token protocol to coordinate station access to the network. It poses a solution to the growing congestion of older networks brought about by the increased use of high-performance workstations, servers, graphics interfaces, and multimedia applications.

This book describes the features, topologies, and components of the FDDI standards. It was prepared by members of the Networking and Communications Marketing and Engineering groups of Digital Equipment Corporation and originally published through Digital's Telecommunications and Networks Publications as *A Primer to FDDI: Fiber Distributed Data Interface*. The *Primer* was a response to the rising interest in FDDI shown by computer system managers, telecommunications managers, and others whose professional responsibilities included linked computer systems.

Because interest in FDDI continues to grow, Digital Press is making a nonproprietary version of the updated *Primer* available to a wider audience through traditional book-selling channels. This book should appeal to readers who want an introduction to FDDI technology without reference to a particular set of products. It should be especially valuable to communications professionals involved with networks and network implementation, and consultants and support professionals for organizations that need to expand existing networks.

Acknowledgments

This book was developed and produced through the collaboration of a number of organizations and disciplines. The following individuals contributed to its content: Chris Baldwin, Paul Callahan, Tom Gulick, James Kuenzel, Diana Larrea, Karen Leonard, Jonathan Levy, James Marsh, John Swan, and Karen Yim. Dorothy C. Robinson, Alice Phalen, Margo Grant, and Judi Harris provided project management.

In addition, members of the Telecommunications and Networks Publications Group played a major role in bringing the book to market: Phil Dussault, cover design and illustrations; Paul Boccelli, Roland Boisvert, Ben Day, Bob Marsocci, and Casey Scalzi, technical writing; Janet Gubbay, technical editing; and Janet Reddy-Guerette, publications supervisor. Sue Ann McConnaughey of Digital's IDC Publications assisted with the production of the revised edition and the Digital Press version.

Conventions Used in This Book

• Words and phrases defined in the glossary appear in italics in the text.

Key to Symbols

• The following symbols are used in figures throughout this book.

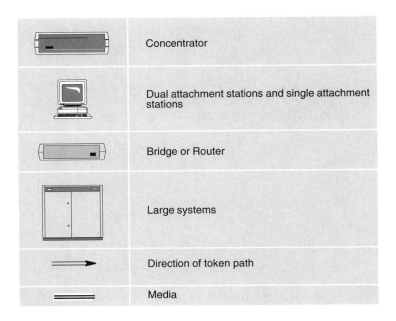

	Concentrator
	Dual attachment stations and single attachment stations
	Bridge or Router
	Large systems
	Direction of token path
	Media

Chapter 1 • FDDI: A New LAN Standard

In today's high-pressure business environment, acquiring and distributing information quickly is critical to the functioning of most companies. Networks play an increasingly important role in this process. Choosing the right network, however, is not always an easy task.

Many factors need to be taken into consideration when building a network. Proprietary networks, nonstandard applications, and single-vendor hardware sourcing, for example, combine to make the job of building networks difficult. Networking standards such as *Fiber Distributed Data Interface* (FDDI) help to simplify this task.

• Network Architecture

Network systems are designed in layers. Each layer performs a special set of functions and services. When you combine the layers, you have a network architecture. A network's architecture is important because it sorts communication functions into logical groups (layers) so that they always perform in a *peer-to-peer* (nonhierarchical) relationship.

Protocols

Each layer has its own set of rules and procedures called *protocols*. Protocols regulate activity within the layer. They also regulate communication and transfer of data between layers and across links between *nodes*. The layers are independent of each other; that is, changes in one layer do not affect operations or protocols in neighboring layers. For example, changing the physical transmission medium does not affect the type of data link.

This layered approach means that:

* Designing networks and network functions is easier.

* Networks can provide users with a greater range of accessible and easy-to-use capabilities such as distributed databases and applications.

* Upgrades are easier to implement.

• Open Systems Interconnection

The *Open Systems Interconnection* (OSI) Reference Model is a seven-layer representation of an open network architecture. The ability to move information between multivendor equipment is referred to as *interoperability* or open communications. The Open Systems Interconnection Reference Model provides a framework for the development of international standards for computer communications. These standards provide the basis for multivendor interoperability.

• The OSI Reference Model

The OSI model shown in Figure 1 was developed by the *International Organization for Standardization* (ISO) and the *International Telegraph and Telephone Consultative Committee* (CCITT).

Only layers 1, 2, and 3 are described here since they are pertinent to discussing FDDI networking.

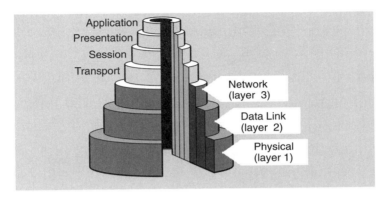

Figure 1 • The OSI Reference Model

The Physical Layer

The *Physical layer* (layer 1) specifies the electrical and physical connections between systems. This layer also specifies signaling in a format that is compatible with the medium used (for example, coaxial cable or fiber). This operation is called *encoding*.

The Data Link Layer

The *Data Link layer* (layer 2) introduces control information into messages that are to be transmitted. This layer also defines:

- *Frame* construction

- Data Link addressing

- Error detection

- Access rules for the network

The Network Layer

The *Network layer* (layer 3) permits communications between network nodes in an open network. This layer:

- Provides network-wide node addressing

- Provides mechanisms to route frames between similar or dissimilar networks

• The OSI Reference Model and Interconnect Devices

Repeaters, bridges, and routers link networks together. They are referred to as interconnect devices.

Repeaters

The simplest network interconnect device is a *repeater* (Figure 2). ISO documents call a repeater a physical relay or level 1 relay. Repeaters perform no Data Link functions.

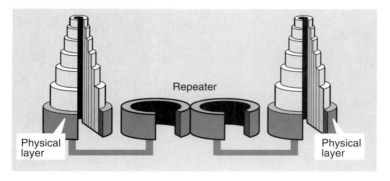

Figure 2 • Repeaters operate at layer 1

A repeater acts on the bits transferred between segments of the same Physical layers. It repeats, re-times, and amplifies the bits so that the distance between nodes can be extended. Note that a repeater is limited to connecting one or more cable segments between communicating nodes. When a repeater is used, the Data Link protocols must be identical for communication between the nodes to be successful.

Bridges

A *bridge* links similar or dissimilar LANs together to form an *extended LAN*. ISO documents call a bridge a Data Link relay or level 2 relay (Figure 3). Bridges act on the frames transferred between the Data Link layers of two nodes, while repeaters act on the bits transferred between Physical layers.

Bridges are designed to store and then forward frames destined for another LAN; local traffic remains local. They are also protocol independent, thus allowing any protocol such as DECnet, Transmission Control Protocol (TCP)/Internet Protocol (IP), Internet Packet Exchange (IPX), and LAT to traverse the bridge.

Ideally, bridges are invisible (transparent) to the end-stations that are communicating through the bridge. The end-station does not know that the bridge exists or that the message is going through the bridge.

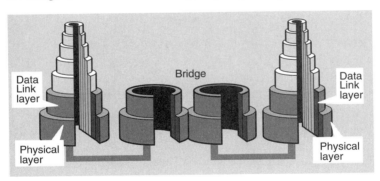

Figure 3 • Bridges operate at layers 1 and 2

Routers

Routers were originally designed for low-speed wide-area links but are now also used to link LANs. ISO documents call a router an *intermediate system*, network relay, or level 3 relay (Figure 4). Routers are Network layer (layer 3) devices.

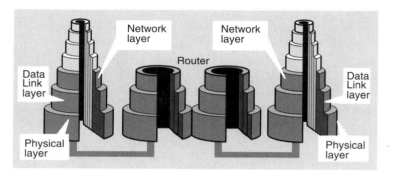

Figure 4 • *Routers operate at layers 1, 2, and 3*

Routers act on the frames transferred between the Network layers of two nodes. Bridges act on the frames transferred between the Data Link layers of two nodes. Repeaters act on the bits transferred between the Physical layers of two network segments.

Routers are known to the end-station; bridges are transparent to the end-station. Nodes periodically send messages to the router confirming their existence and their address. The router keeps a record of node addresses and current network status. It forwards a message directly to a local or remote LAN over the route with the least amount of traffic or lowest cost, as defined by the network manager.

Routers isolate LANs into subnetworks that can manage and contain network traffic. For example, traffic containment is useful in some environments where the protocols used can cause unnecessary network congestion *(for example, broadcast storms).*

• What LANs Do

LANs connect computers, terminals, and other equipment within a limited geographical area. Bridges and routers connect LANs over distances that exceed the capabilities of a single LAN. Such a configuration is called an extended LAN.

OSI standards allow different types of LANs to be linked together. For example, two *IEEE* 802.3 networks can be connected with an 802.3/Ethernet bridge or router (Figure 5). Additionally, LANs can be linked to *wide area networks* (WANs) to create an enterprise network.

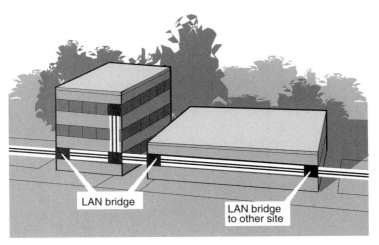

LAN bridge

LAN bridge to other site

Figure 5 • Extended LANs

• Defining Fiber Distributed Data Interface

Fiber Distributed Data Interface (FDDI) is a set of LAN standards. FDDI was developed under the procedures of the *American National Standards Institute* (ANSI). The standards have also been approved for international use by the ISO. FDDI offers an industry-standard solution for organizations that need flexible, robust, high-performance networks.

FDDI is a 100 Mb/s timed *token-passing* LAN. It is constructed of two independent counter rotating rings that are connected together in case of ring faults. FDDI can connect up to 500 stations for a total fiber distance of 200 kilometers. The FDDI standards provide for manageability, high speed, low-error rates, and high fault tolerance.

Multimode fiber-optic cable was the first transmission medium defined in the FDDI standard, followed by the standard for *single-mode* fiber-optic cable. Support for copper media is under development by the ANSI Committee.

The following ANSI standards define the components of FDDI:

- *Physical Layer Medium Dependent* (PMD) standards define the medium and the connectors for multimode and single-mode fiber-optic cable.

- *Physical Layer Protocol* (PHY) standard defines the rules for encoding of data.

- *Media Access Control* (MAC) standard defines the protocols for operation of the token ring and construction of frames and tokens.

- *Station Management* (SMT) standard defines the protocols for managing the PMD, PHY, and MAC entities.

The FDDI standards also define several types of networking devices. These include *concentrators*, *Dual Attachment Stations*, and *Single Attachment Stations*:

- Concentrators are a basic building block of an FDDI network. They are so named because they concentrate or gather together several lines in one central location. They attach directly to the FDDI dual *ring* — that is, to the primary and secondary ring. Concentrators provide highly fault tolerant connections to the ring.

- Dual Attachment Station (DAS) devices connect directly to the dual ring or to a concentrator.

- Single Attachment Station (SAS) devices connect to the ring only through a concentrator.

These devices allow you to create customized network configurations based on the FDDI standards (Figure 6).

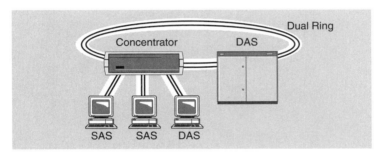

Figure 6 • FDDI networking devices
The FDDI standards specify:

- Fiber-optic cable type (described in Chapter 3)
  – 62.5/125 micron multimode fiber
  – 8–10/125 micron single-mode fiber

- Ring distance as a maximum fiber length of 200 kilometers (124 miles)

- Link distance between stations for
  – multimode fiber with a maximum length of 2 kilometers (1.2 miles)
  – single-mode fiber in excess of 20 kilometers (12.4 miles)

- A maximum of 500 stations per FDDI LAN

• High-Speed LAN Technology

The FDDI 100 Mb/s LAN technology moves large amounts of data. FDDI represents a tenfold increase in speed over the IEEE 802.3 standard, and an even greater increase in speed over the 4 Mb/s IEEE 802.5 standard. No single technology alone meets the demand for *bandwidth* and number of end-user connections. FDDI coexists with and complements current LAN standards, representing a component part of LAN integration (Figure 7).

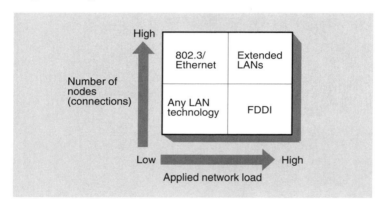

Figure 7 • Integration of LAN technologies

• Need for FDDI

Why do we need another LAN standard? Network planners and analysts see the potential for severe network bottlenecks occurring now and in the near future. Reasons for the network congestion can be attributed to the increasing:

• Number of users being added to the network

• Computing power of desktop systems

• Business needs for more complex networks spanning longer distances

• Traffic loads on existing backbone networks

• Number of client/server facilities

In addition to these reasons, other factors made the development of a new, high-speed LAN a necessity. For example:

• The requirement for networks to support graphics-intensive applications

• The increase in multimedia applications

FDDI is a standards-based solution to this problem. Current LANs are limited to data transfer rates in the range of 4 to 16 Mb/s. However, FDDI has a data transfer rate of 100 Mb/s over longer distances. FDDI uses the high bandwidth provided by *fiber optics* and advanced product designs.

FDDI is an ideal candidate to act as the backbone that links other LANs together. The increased data transfer rate of FDDI allows the creation of networks that link systems running compute- and graphics-intensive applications.

FDDI is the LAN standard of choice where size, distance, and speed are critical concerns. Because it is a standard that has been extensively accepted by the computer industry, multivendor availability is assured.

• Summary

A network architecture consists of several layers, each with its own set of protocols that regulate the transfer of data between layers and between nodes. The Open Systems Interconnection Reference Model is a seven-layer model of a network architecture and is used as the basis for the FDDI standards.

LANs connect computers, terminals, and other equipment in a building or on a campus. Extended LANs are typically created by connecting LANs together with bridges and routers.

FDDI is a set of ANSI/ISO LAN standards that provide a 100 Mb/s data rate and maximum fiber length of 200 kilometers. The current standards are Physical Layer Medium Dependent (PMD), Single-Mode Fiber Physical Layer Medium Dependent (SMF-PMD), Physical Layer Protocol (PHY), Media Access Control (MAC), and Station Management (SMT).

FDDI features a timed token-passing technology and addresses the need for a network that supports increased size, distance, and speed over existing networks.

Chapter 2 • FDDI: A LAN Built to the OSI Model

The Open Systems Interconnection (OSI) Reference Model defines the communications architecture between open systems. The FDDI Interface standards are based on the requirements of the Physical and Data Link layers of the OSI model.

• FDDI and the OSI Model

FDDI divides both the Physical layer and Data Link layer of the OSI Reference Model into sublayers as follows:

- The Physical layer is divided into two sublayers, PMD and PHY:
  - The lower sublayer is defined by Physical Layer Medium Dependent (PMD) standards, which specify requirements such as media and connector types.
  - The upper sublayer is defined in the Physical Layer Protocol (PHY) standard, which specifies transmission details such as line states, clocking requirements, and data encoding rules.

- The Data Link layer is divided into two sublayers, MAC and LLC:
  - The lower sublayer, the FDDI Media Access Control (MAC) standard, defines the FDDI *timed-token protocol*, frame formats, and addressing conventions.

– The upper sublayer is defined in the IEEE 802.2 *Logical Link Control* (LLC) standard. LLC provides a means for exchanging data between LLC users.

The FDDI Station Management (SMT) standard defines how to manage the Physical Layer Medium Dependent, Physical Layer Protocol, and Media Access Control portions of FDDI. It includes mechanisms for establishing communication and ensuring the ring's stability.

Figure 8 shows the relationship between the FDDI standards and the OSI Reference Model.

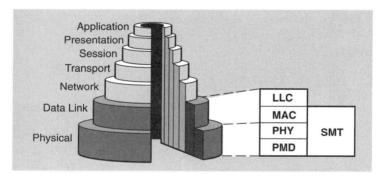

Figure 8 ● *Relationship between the FDDI standards and the OSI Reference Model*

Figure 9 shows the relationship among the various FDDI standards and how they combine to form the complete FDDI specification.

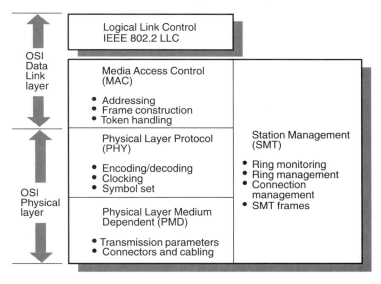

Figure 9 • Relationship among the FDDI standards

• FDDI Concepts

FDDI is a token passing LAN technology that utilizes a timed-token protocol. This protocol guarantees that stations will gain access to the ring within a time period that is negotiated between the stations each time a new station joins the ring.

An FDDI ring is constructed of nodes, which connect together via links to form the ring. The nodes can be of two types: Dual Attachment Stations and Single Attachment Stations. A special type of node, called a Concentrator, allows connection of stations into the ring, and provides for greater fault tolerance than the basic ring architecture.

One of the important features of FDDI is the use of dual counter rotating rings. The dual rings are independent until a fault (such as a cable break) occurs, in which case the rings are joined together, or wrapped, in order to restore the ring to its operational state.

FDDI is based on the use of fiber-optic technology, which allows rings with a total fiber length of 200 kilometers to be constructed. Using multimode fiber, interstation distances of 2 kilometers are permitted while single-mode fiber implementations enable interstation distances that exceed 20 kilometers. Future enhancements to the FDDI standard will allow the use of cost-reduced fiber optics for runs less than 500 meters, and *twisted pair* cable for runs of up to 100 meters.

ANSI and ASC X3T9 Committee

ANSI defines and oversees the standards creation process for the United States. Committees and task groups develop and write the standards that are then approved and issued in accordance with ANSI procedures.

The Accredited Standards Committee (ASC) X3 develops standards for Information Processing Systems. The Technical Committee X3T9 is responsible for writing standards for I/O interfaces. The ASC X3T9.5 Task Group is chartered by ANSI to write the FDDI standards and is responsible for the design of the overall specification.

The ANSI X3T9 Committee reviewed many options during the FDDI development process. Because of the 100 Mb/s transmission rate, FDDI presented a new set of challenges to designers who were determined to create a reliable, high-speed network. Because of their efforts, FDDI provides reliable transmission services over great distances among large numbers of stations.

There has been multivendor participation in the development of the FDDI standards. This means the standard is not associated with a particular vendor, thus ensuring multivendor interoperability.

• Industry Standard LAN Technologies

Table 1 lists the ANSI/ISO reference documents and summarizes each standard. The following chapters discuss each of these standards (including those that are currently under development) in nontechnical terms. For detailed technical information, refer to the individual ANSI or ISO document for each standard.

Table 1 • ANSI and ISO standards for FDDI

ANSI/ISO Standard	FDDI Standard
PMD: X3.166–1990/ ISO 9314-3:1990 SMF–PMD: X3.184–1991 LCF–PMD: TBD TP–PMD: TBD	**Physical Layer Medium Dependent**—Four standards correspond to the lower portion of the OSI Physical layer and define the transmit/receive power levels, transmitter and receiver interface requirements, error rates, and cable and connector specifications (see Chapter 3). These standards are: • Physical Layer Medium Dependent (PMD) • Single-Mode Fiber Physical Layer Medium Dependent (SMF–PMD) • Low-Cost Fiber Physical Layer Medium Dependent (LCF–PMD)-under development • Twisted Pair Physical Layer Medium Dependent (TP–PMD)-under development
X3.148–1988/ ISO 9314-1:1989	**Physical Layer Protocol**—This medium-independent standard corresponds to the upper portion of the Physical layer. PHY defines symbols, line states, encoding/decoding techniques, clocking requirements, and data framing requirements (see Chapter 4).
X3.139–1987/ ISO 9314-2:1989	**Media Access Control**—This standard corresponds to the lower portion of the OSI Data Link layer. MAC defines data link addressing, frame formatting, media access, error detecting, and token handling (see Chapter 5).
X3T9.5/84–49	**Station Management**—This standard defines the system management services for the FDDI protocols. SMT includes facilities for connection management, node configuration, recovery from error conditions, and the encoding of SMT frames (see Chapter 6).

Three other popular LAN standards have ISO approval: IEEE 802.3, IEEE 802.4, and IEEE 802.5.

Figure 10 shows the relationship between the FDDI standards and other industry-standard LAN technologies. Note that the IEEE 802.2 Logical Link Control and IEEE 802.1 standards are common across the various lower layer standards. IEEE 802.1d, for example, is a standard for bridging LANs.

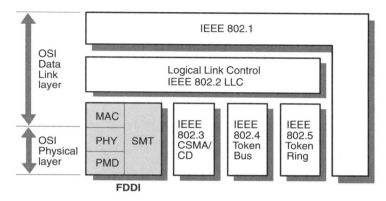

Figure 10 • Relationship between FDDI and other LAN standards

• Design Concepts

The ANSI FDDI standards and the IEEE 802.2 LLC standard provide for essential networking services to stations attached to the FDDI network. These services include hardware connection, ring initialization, frame construction, error detection, token handling, and overall station management.

Figure 11 shows the relationship of the FDDI sublayer entities.

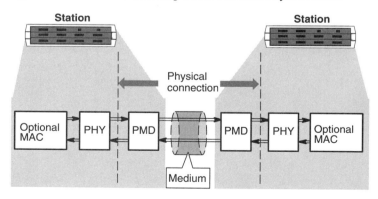

Figure 11 • FDDI sublayer entities

Aside from these basic services, FDDI offers a number of features not found in other LAN technologies. These features include, but are not limited to, the following:

- Dual counter-rotating ring topology to aid fault recovery

- 100 Mb/s transmission rate

- A maximum length of 2 kilometers (1.24 miles) between stations using multimode fiber and distances in excess of 20 kilometers (12.4 miles) between stations using single-mode fiber

- A total fiber length of 200 kilometers (124 miles)

- Sophisticated encoding techniques to ensure data integrity

- Distributed clocking to support a large number of stations on the ring

FDDI offers advanced design and technology, and is a feature-rich, powerful networking standard geared to provide reliable data transmission at high speeds.

• Application Environments

FDDI supports various LAN configurations including *workgroup*, *backbone,* and *backend* networks. These configurations provide great flexibility in the design and implementation of an FDDI network.

FDDI Workgroup Configuration

A workgroup configuration is characterized by a relatively small number of attached devices spread over a limited geographical area. A workgroup configuration connects workstations, servers, and mini-computers through one or more FDDI concentrators.

Figure 12, Figure 13, and Figure 14 illustrate FDDI workgroup environments using concentrators. See Chapter 9 for more information about workgroup configurations.

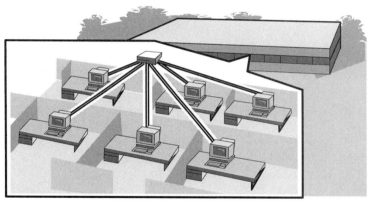

Figure 12 • Workgroup environment

FDDI Backbone Configuration

The FDDI backbone provides a high-bandwidth facility to link multiple LANs in a campus or a building into an integrated network as shown in Figure 13 and Figure 14. Designed for high reliability, the FDDI backbone configuration supports radial wiring topologies as defined by the *Electronic Industries Association/Telecommunications Industries Association* (EIA/TIA) 568 standard for commercial building wiring, as well as dual rings.

Building 1

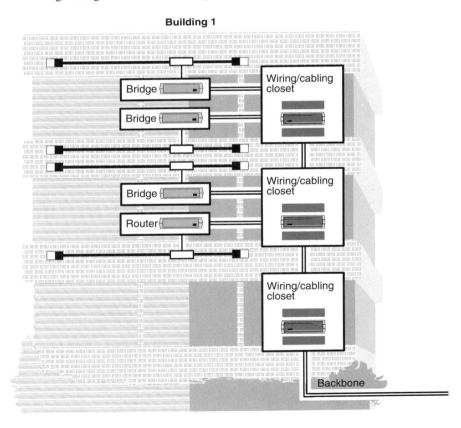

Figure 13 • FDDI backbone configuration

Devices connect to the FDDI LAN either directly or through a concentrator. The use of concentrators maintains ring integrity even when one or all devices attached to it are off line. This means that users can power down the attached devices without disrupting the FDDI network. In the FDDI backbone configuration shown in Figure 13, the network is able to sustain the loss of one or more attached nodes and still function reliably.

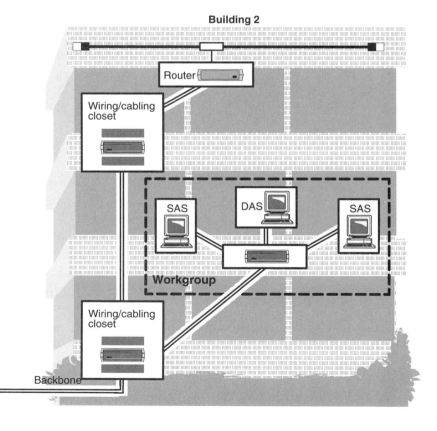

FDDI Backend Configuration

Given its high bandwidth capability, FDDI is ideally suited for network connections between large systems (host-to-host) or between large systems and peripheral devices, such as disk farms that are either co-located or remotely located from one another. Using optical fiber, FDDI's extended distance capability enables backend configurations

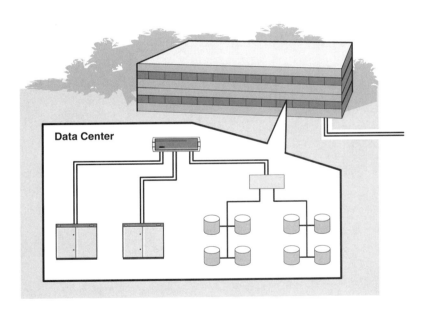

Figure 14 • FDDI backend configuration

to span multiple floors in a building and multiple buildings in a campus environment. The hosts and disk farms attach to the FDDI LAN with or without a concentrator. Figure 14 expands upon the backbone and workgroup configurations to include mainframes and disk farms, enabling users in both facilities to share systems and resources across the FDDI network.

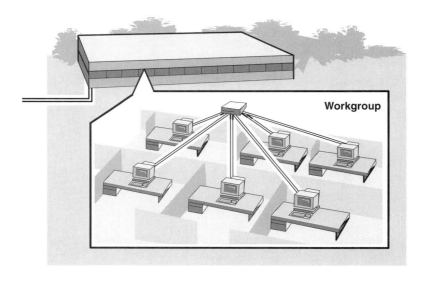

Workgroup

• Fiber-Optic Cable

Multimode and single-mode fiber-optic cables are the current standardized media defined in the FDDI standards. The ANSI committee for FDDI is also considering twisted pair media.

Fiber-optic cable offers:

• High bandwidth for transmission of data over long distances

• Immunity to electromagnetic and radio frequency interference

• Security

High Bandwidth, Low Loss, and Long Distance

High bandwidth and low loss over relatively long distances are major features of fiber-optic cable.

Bandwidth is a measure of the amount of data a medium can carry, usually expressed in cycles per second or Hertz. It is sometimes used interchangeably with capacity, which is also a measure of the amount of data a medium can carry. Capacity is expressed in bits per second: FDDI specifies a capacity or bandwidth of 100 Megabits per second or Mb/s.

Loss (*attenuation*) bounds how far a signal can travel before it can no longer be recognized by the receiving device. Because fiber characteristically has low loss levels, stations can be spaced much further apart than devices attached to copper cable. This means that fiber is a good choice when the combination of high bandwidth and long distance is needed.

Immunity

Fiber-optic cable transports optical power from point to point. Electromagnetic noise and radio frequency noise have no adverse effect on optical signals, so error rates are inherently low.

Security

Optical fiber provides more protection from unwanted tapping or electronic eavesdropping than any other type of medium. Tapping into a fiber-optic cable without some indication that a break has occurred requires skill and complicated equipment. It can be done, but it is hard to accomplish and fairly easy to detect. Also, because fiber does not emit radio waves, an electronic listening device is ineffective.

• Summary

The FDDI standards address the requirements of the Physical and Data Link layers of the OSI Reference Model. The PMD, PHY, MAC, and SMT standards, along with the IEEE 802.2 LLC standard, provide essential networking services to devices attached to an FDDI network.

FDDI design concepts include a dual-ring architecture, 100 Mb/s data rate, and sophisticated encoding techniques to support a large number of stations on the ring.

FDDI supports LAN configurations such as a backbone, stand-alone workgroup, or backend configurations. With the use of concentrators, an FDDI LAN can sustain the loss of one or more attached nodes and still function reliably.

Two types of fiber-optic cable (multimode and single-mode) are defined by the FDDI standards. Fiber is an ideal choice for high-bandwidth applications where electromagnetic interference or security is of concern.

As the standards have matured and the hardware has become readily available, FDDI has emerged as the high-bandwidth LAN standard that meets users' growing network needs.

Chapter 3 • FDDI Technology: PMD Standards

The lowest level of the OSI model is the Physical layer. This level defines the transmission of bits on the physical medium. As shown in Figure 15, FDDI standards subdivide this OSI Physical layer into two sublayers: Physical Layer Medium Dependent (PMD) and Physical Layer Protocol (PHY). These two sublayers separate the physical medium and the transmission details into two distinct parts.

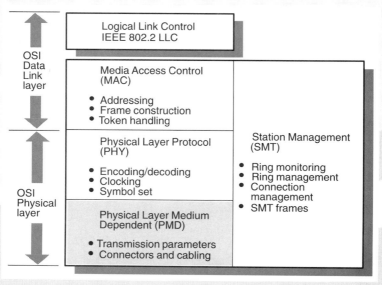

Figure 15 • PMD sublayer

• PMD Standards

FDDI has standardized two PMDs with two others in development by X3T9.5. As highlighted in Figure 15, PMD standards define how nodes *(stations)* physically attach to the FDDI ring and how stations are physically interconnected on the network by media type (optical fiber or copper).

The four types of PMD are:

- PMD—Uses light emitting diodes (LEDs) and multimode fiber. It was the first PMD developed by ANSI.

- SMF-PMD —Uses laser diodes and single-mode fiber. It is used to interconnect stations separated by distances that exceed the 2 kilometers limit imposed by the PMD.

- LCF-PMD —Currently in development by ANSI, the *low-cost fiber* PMD also uses LEDs and multimode fiber. It spans 500 meters between stations and is envisioned to be a lower cost solution than the PMD.

- TP-PMD —Also currently in development, the twisted pair PMD will operate over copper media —*Shielded Twisted Pair* (STP) and some categories of *Unshielded Twisted Pair* (UTP). It is anticipated that the transmission distance between stations will be limited to 100 meters.

• PMD Functions

Data is transmitted between stations by first converting the data bits into a series of signals, then transmitting these signals over the cable linking the two stations. The PMD standards deal with all the areas that are associated with physically transmitting the data:

- Optical and electrical transmitters and receivers

- Fiber-optic or copper cable

- Media interface connector

• Optical bypass relay (optional in optical PMDs)

The PMD standards ensure that the transmitters, cabling, and receivers will interoperate when the specified parameters are properly implemented.

Transmitters and Receivers

The transmitter converts the encoded data (in electrical signals) from the PHY to a series of signals that are used to transmit the data over the medium. The receiver converts the received signals back to electrical signals for communication to the PHY.

Transmitters for Optical Media

Optical transmitters convert modulated electrical signals into modulated light signals. The light signal is then launched into the optical fiber.

The PMD and LCF-PMD specify the parameters for use of a light emitting diode as the optical transmitter. LEDs are usually used with multimode fiber-optic cables, which are described later in this chapter.

The SMF-PMD specifies the parameters for use of laser diodes (LDs) as the optical transmitter.

Receivers for Optical Signals

Optical receivers contain a photodetector that converts the incoming optical signal back into an electrical signal.

One important property of an optical receiver is its *sensitivity*. Receiver sensitivity is the minimum power that an incoming optical signal must have for the receiver to work. The sensitivity of a receiver is maintained only over a limited range of optical wavelengths.

Transmitters and Receivers for Copper Media

The transmitters and receivers for the copper media are conventional line drivers and receivers. The simplicity of these components is one of the reasons for the expected low cost of this transmission technology.

Fiber-Optic Cable

The PMD standards specify size and optical characteristics for the fiber-optic cable in the following areas:

• Wavelength of the optical signal that transmits the data

• Attenuation (amount of power loss) in the cable

• Type of cable (the fiber medium)

Nominal Optical Wavelength

Nominal optical wavelength refers to the approximate wavelength of the light rays used to transmit data over the fiber-optic cable. Light sources emit light in a specific set of colors (or wavelengths). Wavelengths are expressed in nanometers (nm).

• Optical transmitters specified by FDDI emit light at or near a nominal wavelength of 1300 nm.

As shown in Figure 16, the optical power emitted by a transmitter is spread over a range of wavelengths. The nominal optical wavelength is sometimes referred to as the center wavelength. The range can be narrow or wide depending on the type of light source: LD or LED.

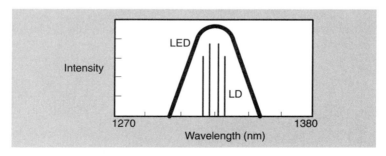

Figure 16 • Optical wavelengths of LED and LD transmitters

Operating Wavelength and Windows

Not all light waves travel over optical fiber with the same degree of efficiency. For example, the attenuation (loss) of light signals is higher for visible light than for the near-infrared region. Visible light has wavelengths from 400 to 700 nm while the near-infrared region has wavelengths from 700 to 1600 nm.

In the near-infrared region, there are several wavelengths that travel over optical fiber with very little loss. These wavelengths are most suitable for optical communication and are called *windows*. The most common windows are 850 nm, 1300 nm, and 1550 nm.

Multimode fibers operate at 850 nm (first window), 1300 nm (second window) or both 850 nm and 1300 nm (dual window). The use of dual-window fiber in an installation provides support for current as well as future needs. Single-mode fiber is designed to operate at a wavelength of 1300 nm and/or 1550 nm.

Attenuation

Attenuation describes the amount of optical power that is lost as the light travels from the transmitter through the cable to the receiver. Power loss is expressed in *decibels* (dB). A decibel is a mathematical expression used to compare the power of two signals.

The attenuation of a fiber link is calculated by knowing the unit attenuation and the length of the link. Think of unit attenuation as the number of decibels lost as the light travels through a specified length of cable. The longer a cable, the higher the loss of optical power.

The *power budget* of a system is determined by the minimum transmitter power and the minimum receiver sensitivity.

- The FDDI PMD standard specifies a power budget of 11.0 dB and a maximum cable attenuation of 1.5 dB/kilometers at a wavelength of 1300 nm.

Some power is lost as it passes through connectors and splices in the cable. Each splice introduces a specific amount of loss. When an optical system is installed, it is a good idea to plan for several future repair splices.

The total amount of loss that can be introduced and still have the optical system work is called the *link-loss budget*. The link-loss budget is the difference between the minimum transmitter power and the receiver sensitivity minus any allowance for repair splices and future connectors.

The maximum attenuation allowed for the cable is determined by subtracting the losses of all the splices and connectors from the link-loss budget.

- The FDDI SMF-PMD specifies a range of permissible power budgets. The range is dependent on the types of transmitters employed and extends from a minimum of 10 dB to a maximum of 32 dB.

Type of Cable

The PMD and SMF-PMD standards specify the type of cable used as the transmission medium for an FDDI network. Concepts associated with multimode (PMD) and single-mode (SMF-PMD) optical-fiber specifications are described in the following sections.

Core and Cladding Diameters

Optical fibers consist of a central core glass cylinder surrounded by a cladding glass tube. Optical fiber is usually referred to by its core and cladding diameters (Figure 17). For example, fiber with a core diameter of 62.5 micrometers (microns) and a cladding diameter of 125 microns is referred to as a 62.5/125 micron fiber. Three sizes of multimode fiber are commonly used today: 62.5/125 micron, 50/125 micron, and 100/140 micron.

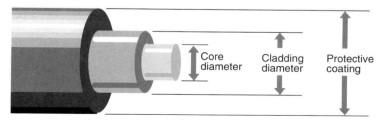

Figure 17 • Optical fiber

The actual optical medium consists of the core and the cladding. The outer coating plus any jacketing, if used, encloses the fiber to form a protective barrier against possible damage.

The core is formed of *doped* glass and transmits the data by carrying optical energy between devices. The cladding that surrounds the core is also a type of optical glass and is designed to reflect light waves back into the core. Material used for the cladding is doped differently than material used for the core.

Index Profile

The chemical composition of glass produces an optical property called the *refractive index*. The refractive index is a measure of the speed of light in the material relative to the speed of light in a vacuum. The core and cladding each have a different refractive index. The core always has a higher refractive index than the cladding. The *index profile* is the refractive index as a function of distance from the core center.

Step-Index Fiber

When the refractive index of the core material is uniform, the fiber is called a *step-index* fiber because of the sudden change of the refractive index at the core-cladding boundary.

Each light ray traveling in the cable is referred to as a mode. The speed of the light rays traveling through step-index fiber is uniform. However, as described later in this chapter, the variation in the direction of the path of the light rays results in quite different arrival times at the end of the fiber. This produces high levels of optical pulse broadening, and limits the speed at which data can pass through the fiber. Step-index, multimode fiber has very low-bandwidth characteristics and is not permitted by the PMD.

Graded-Index Fiber

The high levels of optical pulse broadening and low bandwidth can be corrected by varying the core refractive index so that:

• It is high at the center

• Matches the cladding refractive index at the core-cladding boundary

This fiber type is called a *graded-index* fiber and is the approved FDDI multimode fiber. The index profile of graded-index fiber is nearly parabolic. Consequently, the speed of light rays traveling through different parts of the fiber is not a constant. This effect compensates for the different path directions of the modes (rays) and reduces the difference in their travel times. The result is less pulse broadening and thus increased bandwidth. Higher bandwidths are achievable over multimode, graded-index fiber than over multimode, step-index fiber.

Travel of Light Rays Through Fiber

The ability to transmit light waves depends on the angle that light enters the fiber. Think of the transmitter as having a light source placed right up against a cone. As shown in Figure 18, the light spreads out as it passes through the cone.

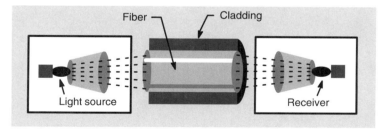

Figure 18 • Light waves striking fiber

Light entering the fiber strikes the core-cladding junction at different points and angles. The light then takes multiple paths of varying lengths to the end connection.

Figure 19 is an example of light traveling through a fiber. As shown in the figure, ray 1 enters the fiber directly at its center, then travels through the center directly to the end connection.

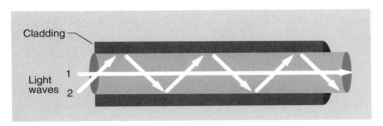

Figure 19 • Light traveling through step-index fiber

Ray 2 enters the fiber at a different angle and follows a reflected path to the end connection. This is similar to something ricocheting through a tube. When the different light rays exit at the other end, they combine to give a light pulse that is:

• Reduced in amplitude

• Wider (in duration) than the pulse that entered the fiber

Graded-index fibers are designed to minimize these effects.

Mode Capacity
Fibers can be multimode or single-mode.

Multimode Fiber Characteristics
Multimode means that multiple modes (or rays) can be transmitted over the fiber at the same time. Typically, multimode fiber has a core diameter of 50, 62.5, or 100 microns.

Multimode fiber has varying light transmission capabilities and can be either step index or graded index. When fiber is used in FDDI applications, the specifications recommend 62.5 micron, graded-index multimode fiber. Step-index multimode does not meet the FDDI bandwidth requirements and thus is not allowed.

Single-Mode Fiber Characteristics

Single-mode fiber can also be used in FDDI applications, particularly for long-distance applications. Called monomode fiber in Europe, single-mode means that only one mode of transmission (or ray) is propagated in the fiber. Single-mode fiber has a much smaller core than multimode fiber. Typically, single-mode fibers have a core diameter between 8 and 10 microns and cladding diameters of 125 microns.

Single-mode fiber is used almost exclusively with laser light sources. The chromatic characteristics of the laser combined with the larger bandwidth of single-mode fiber permit long transmission distances at the high FDDI data rate.

Copper Media

The ANSI X3T9.5 Committee has a formal project underway to develop a TP-PMD standard for transmitting 100 Mb/s data using twisted-pair—both shielded (STP) and unshielded (UTP)—copper cable.

Several quality levels of UTP exist, accommodating various voice and data transmission rates. EIA/TIA, UL (Underwriters Laboratory), and NEMA (National Electrical Manufacturers) are standardizing UTP cable categories or levels.

Categories 1 and 2 are typically used for voice and low-speed data transmission rates, for example RS232. The following list shows the categories that are significant to FDDI users, with corresponding voice and data transmission rates typically supported by each:

- Category 3: up to and including 10 Mb/s (10BaseT)

- Category 4: up to and including 16 Mb/s (16 Mb/s token rings)

- Category 5: up to and including 100 Mb/s (FDDI)

Considerable work at the ANSI standards level remains to be done at the time of this writing because support for FDDI signaling over UTP is considerably more difficult than support over other copper media. The susceptibility of UTP to environmental interference varies with UTP type. There is greater difficulty in meeting FCC (and other) regulations for emissions. The signal carrying properties of the various cable categories are quite different. In general, the challenge is greater in finding a uniform and viable solution for UTP than other copper media. Thus, the ANSI committee is faced with defining solutions in the following areas:

- Determining the UTP categories that will be supported

- Determining achievable distances

- Satisfying emissions regulatory requirements (for example, FCC)

- Selecting an encoding scheme(s) for FDDI signaling

Media Interface Connector

The ANSI standards define the methods for physically connecting a cable to an FDDI station. The *media interface connector* (MIC) for the PMD standard is shown in Figure 20 and is used to connect multimode fiber to an FDDI station.

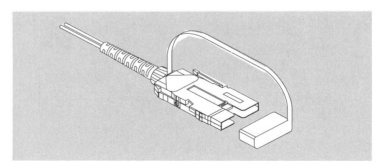

Figure 20 • Media interface connector with cover

The MIC properly aligns the fiber with the transmit/receive optics in the station. The connector consists of a keyed plug and a keyed receptacle. The MIC is polarized to ensure proper transmit/receive-to-fiber association. FDDI MICs can be fitted with keys that define the type of port to which the MIC connects.

ST-type connectors are also commonly used to physically connect optical fiber to an FDDI station. FDDI stations designed for ST-type rather than MIC connections typically provide a lower cost alternative. Care, however, must be taken to ensure that transmit and receive connections are not reversed, since ST-type connectors do not provide a polarized receptacle.

The SMF-PMD allows both a SMF MIC (which closely resembles the connector in Figure 20) as well as other connectors. One such example is an FC-PC connector. The LCF-PMD specifies a duplex SC connector. The connectors for the TP-PMD are still in development.

FDDI Port Types

The ANSI FDDI standards specify connection rules to ensure against the construction of illegal topologies. In the FDDI topology, there are four port types: A, B, M, and S. Figure 21 shows the various ports used in FDDI. The mechanical keying of the connector is defined by the PMD standard.

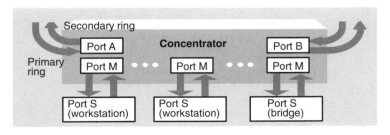

Figure 21 • *Port types used in FDDI*

- Port A connects to the incoming primary ring and the outgoing secondary ring of the FDDI dual ring. This port is part of a Dual Attachment Station (DAS) or a *Dual Attachment Concentrator* (DAC).

- Port B connects to the outgoing primary ring and the incoming secondary ring of the FDDI dual ring. This port is part of a DAS or a DAC and is also used to connect a DAS to a concentrator.

- Port M connects a concentrator to a Single Attachment Station (SAS), DAS, or another concentrator (DAC or *Single Attachment Concentrator* [SAC]). This port is only implemented in a concentrator (DAC, SAC).

- Port S connects a SAS or a SAC to a concentrator (DAC, SAC).

Optical Bypass Relay

The optical *bypass* relay (option) shown in Figure 22 can be used to maintain connectivity of the FDDI ring in the absence of power or during fault conditions in a station. The bypass relay allows the light to bypass the optical receiver in the faulty station. In this way, the faulty station is bypassed and the operation of the FDDI ring is maintained.

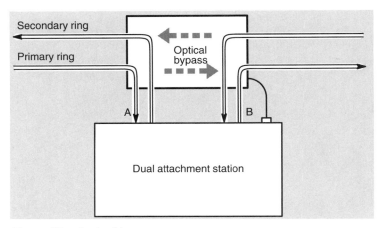

Figure 22 • *Optical bypass*

Optical bypass relays have a *power penalty*, however, which may cause the maximum allowable loss between stations to be exceeded. This limits the number of serially connected relays in the ring.

Other considerations when using optical bypass relays include:

- Bypass relays do not perform repeater functions of amplifying and restoring the bit stream.

- By bypassing a station, the new distance between adjacent stations can exceed the maximum allowable value.

- Bypass relays, as mechanical devices, can fail; thus, the integrity of the dual ring depends on the integrity of the bypass relay.

• Summary

The Physical Layer Medium Dependent standards define the physical requirements for attaching stations to the FDDI network. The PMD standards specify the characteristics of the optical and electrical transmitters and receivers, the medium (fiber or copper), the media interface connector, and an optional optical bypass relay. PMDs provide all the services needed to transmit an encoded digital signal between stations.

The PMD and SMF-PMD (Single-Mode Fiber-PMD) are standards today, with the LCF-PMD (Low-Cost Fiber-PMD) under development by ANSI. The fiber medium is described by the following characteristics: operating wavelength, core and cladding diameters, index profile, and mode capacity (multimode or single-mode).

The TP-PMD (Twisted Pair-PMD) is also under development by ANSI for shielded and unshielded twisted pair copper media. Several technical issues such as selection of an encoding scheme, achievable distances, and electromagnetic regulatory requirements remain to be resolved before the TP-PMD standard is finalized.

Chapter 4 • FDDI Technology: PHY Standard

The Physical Layer Protocol (PHY) standard, shown in Figure 23, defines those portions of the Physical layer that are media independent. This allows new media such as twisted pair to be added without the need to change the PHY parameters.

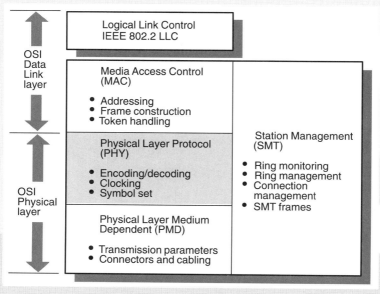

Figure 23 • PHY sublayer

The Physical Layer Protocol defines the following:

- Clock and data recovery—recovers the clock signal from the incoming data.

- Encode/*decode* process—converts data from the MAC into a form for transmission over the FDDI ring.

- Symbols—smallest signaling entities used for communication between stations. Symbols are comprised of 5 *code bits.*

- *Elasticity buffer*—accounts for clock tolerances between stations.

- Smoothing function—prevents frames from being lost due to shortened *preambles.*

- Repeat filter—prevents the propagation of code violations and invalid line states.

• Clock and Data Recovery

The FDDI PHY standard specifies the use of distributed clocking on the network. Each station has a locally generated clock for transmitting or repeating information on the ring.

The receiving station synchronizes its receiver's clock to the incoming symbol stream. The station decodes the data using this clock. When it transmits the data, it uses the local clock as the clock source.

• The Encoding Process

The basic unit of information used in FDDI encoding is the *symbol.* Symbols are used to transmit information between stations on the FDDI network. To transmit frames, the PHY converts the information received from the MAC to an encoded bit stream.

To perform the encoding, FDDI uses both the *4B/5B* and *nonreturn to zero/nonreturn to zero invert on ones* (NRZ/NRZI) encoding schemes. As shown in Figure 24, after a symbol goes through the 4B/5B encoder, it then goes through the NRZ/NRZI encoder.

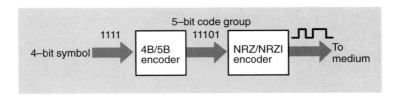

Figure 24 • Encoding

4B/5B Encoding

Using the 4B/5B encoding scheme, the PHY converts the 4-bit symbols into 5-bit *code groups* for transmission over the medium. The 5-bit code groups are chosen to minimize the possible introduction of errors. Note that the use of 5 bits allows for 2^5 or 32 symbols to be transmitted by the PHY.

A device is limited in the number of sequential zero bits it can receive before there are clock reliability problems. To prevent clock problems, each 5-bit code group does not contain more than three zeros in a row.

The use of the 5-bit code groups means that FDDI has a:

* Signaling rate of 125 Megabaud

* Data rate of 100 Mb/s

NRZ/NRZI Encoding

In 4B/5B encoding, five bits were chosen in such a manner as to provide a guaranteed number of transitions to allow for robust clock recovery. This 5-bit code group is further encoded using the NRZI coding scheme.

In this scheme, a transition between power levels indicates a one; no transition indicates a zero. NRZI minimizes the bandwidth required by reducing the number of transitions in the data stream, thus allowing the use of less expensive optical components for the transmitters and receivers.

● Symbols

FDDI defines three types of symbols:

● Data symbols—represent the actual data being sent

● Line state symbols—used for communication between adjacent PHYs

● Control indicator symbols—show the status of the frame

Data Symbols

Of the 32 symbols used in FDDI, only 16 of the 32 represent data. The data is represented in *hexadecimal* form. The remaining symbols define line state and control conditions.

Line State Symbols

Line states are sequences of symbols that are used for PHY signaling. Groups of line state symbols are used to communicate between adjacent PHYs. This adjacent communication is used when the connection begins. Idle symbols are transmitted between frames to aid in clock synchronization.

The receiving PHY determines line states as they are received. Components within SMT use line state symbols to verify and maintain ring integrity.

Control Indicator Symbols

Control indicator symbols are used to indicate the status of a frame. Stations set control symbols as the frame moves around the ring. Some of the status information conveyed by control symbols includes the following:

● Error detected—set by a station that detects an error

● Address recognized—set by a station that recognizes a frame addressed to it

● Frame copied—set by a station that copies the frame

• Elasticity Buffer

Each station uses a locally generated clock to transmit data. While the clock frequencies are tightly controlled, they are never identical. This can cause a repeating station to lose bits as it repeats a frame around the ring. An elasticity buffer is contained in each station to guarantee that frames are not lost due to these clock frequency differences. The elasticity buffer buffers enough bits so that a repeating station always repeats one bit for every bit it receives in a frame.

• Smoothing Function

The start of each FDDI frame has a preamble containing a number of idle symbols. This preamble is used for maintaining synchronization of the receiver clock.

As a frame circles the ring, some symbols in the frame's preamble can be lost. If this occurs, the receiving station can lose the frame. To prevent this, a smoother is built into each PHY.

The smoother inserts or deletes symbols in the preamble before repeating the frame to ensure that enough preamble is present for the *downstream* neighbor to receive the frame.

• Repeat Filter

The repeat filter prevents propagation of code violations and invalid line states. The repeat filter permits:

• Propagation of valid frames

• Propagation of lost (damaged) frames so that they can be counted by the next MAC entity on the ring

• A station to repeat data from its *upstream* neighbor to its downstream neighbor

The repeat filter also includes mechanisms for minimizing the effects of frame fragments, which are partial frames left on the ring by certain MAC operations (see Chapter 7).

• Summary

The PHY standard establishes rules for transmission of symbols on the FDDI ring. It provides the method for clock generation and recovery, and data encoding/decoding. The PHY performs the encoding in two stages: the first is through a 4B/5B encoder; the second is through an NRZ/NRZI encoder.

The basic unit of information in FDDI is the symbol. There are three types of symbols: data symbols that represent hexadecimal data, line state symbols that are used for PHY-level signaling, and control indicator symbols that show the status of a frame.

The elasticity buffer accounts for clock differences between stations, which could otherwise result in loss of frames. The smoothing function of the PHY inserts and deletes symbols at the beginning of a frame to ensure proper reception of the frame by the downstream neighbor. The repeat filter function prevents the propagation of code violations and invalid line states, which assist in isolating errors to a single link.

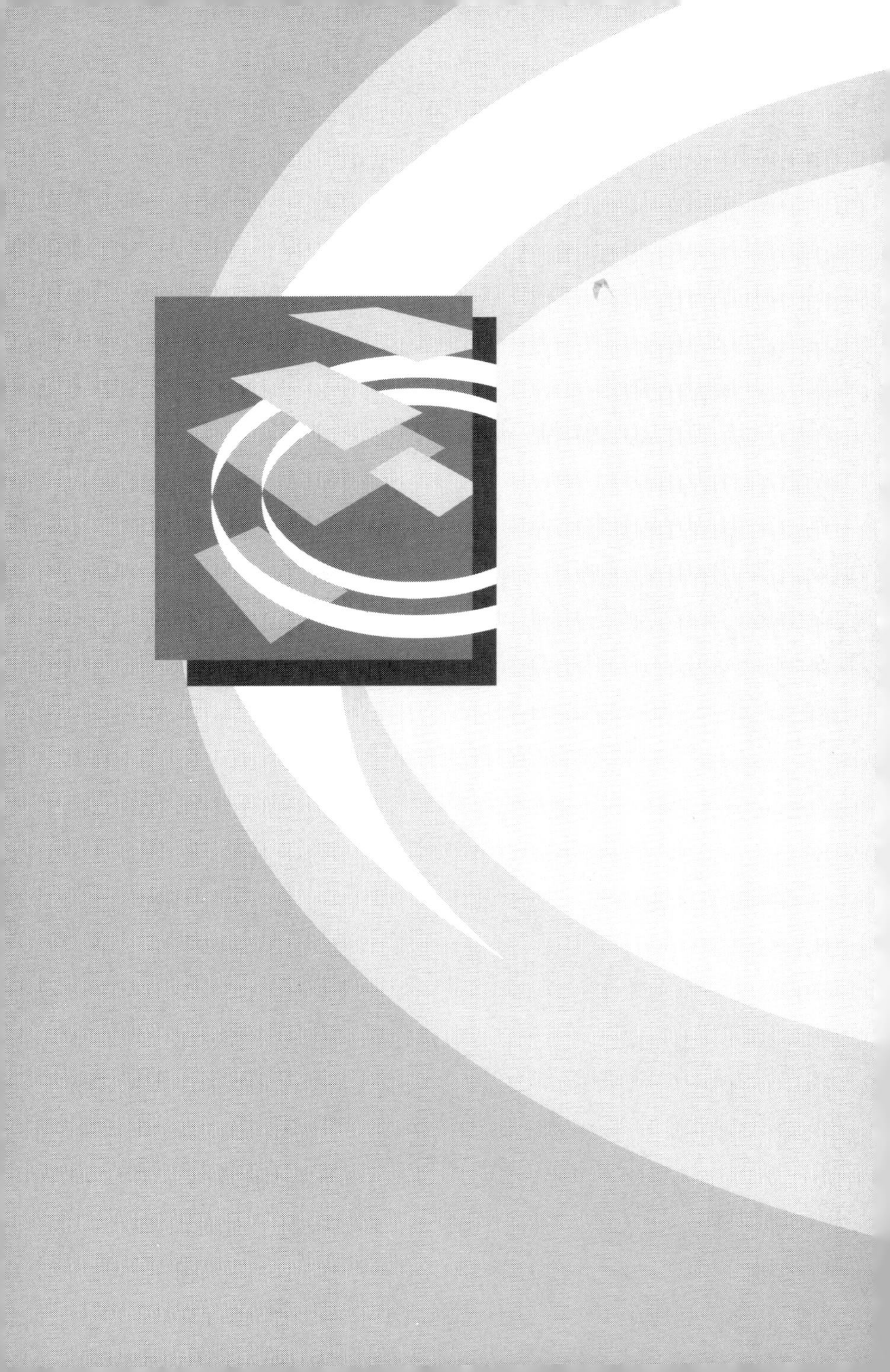

Chapter 5 • FDDI Technology: MAC and LLC Standards

The second level of the OSI Reference Model is the Data Link layer. As shown in Figure 25, the Data Link layer is divided into two sublayers: Media Access Control (MAC) and Logical Link Control (LLC).

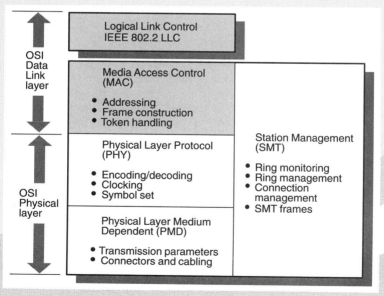

Figure 25 • MAC sublayer

● Media Access Control

The FDDI MAC standard defines the following services:

● Fair and equal access to the ring through use of the timed token protocol

● Communication between attached devices using frames and tokens

● Construction of frames and tokens

● Transmitting, receiving, repeating, and stripping frames and tokens from the ring

● Various error detection mechanisms

● Ring initialization

● Ring fault isolation

NOTE

Although commonly used, the term *MAC-bridge* has no relationship with the FDDI Media Access Control protocols or services. A MAC-bridge simply refers to any Data Link layer bridge.

● Communication on the Ring

As shown in Figure 26, an FDDI ring consists of stations connected in series by medium segments that form a closed loop. Data is transmitted serially as a symbol stream from one attached station to its downstream neighbor. Each station in turn regenerates and *repeats* each symbol, passing the symbol to the next station.

When stations join the ring, the ring is initialized by a bidding process that results in an agreement for a guaranteed service time. The right to transmit data is controlled by a *token,* which is generated by the winner of the bidding process.

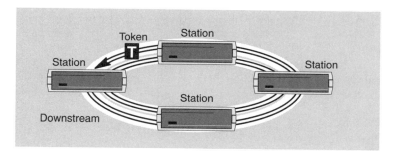

Figure 26 • Stations on an FDDI timed-token ring

The token is passed from one station to another on the FDDI ring. It is a unique symbol sequence that circulates around the ring and is divided into several fields. Each field contains a number of FDDI symbols that define start of token, token type, and end of token.

A station on the ring captures the token when it wants to transmit data. The station then transmits for as long as the token holding rules allow, and reissues the token onto the ring. It reissues the token when it has sent all of its frames, or exhausted its available transmission time. When the frame returns to the sending station, that station removes the frame from the ring via a process called *stripping*.

Ring Scheduling

The fundamental concepts of FDDI include the use of a timed-token protocol (TTP). The TTP defines the rules for acquiring access to the ring. The timed token protocol guarantees that the token appears at a station within twice the *target token rotation time* (TTRT). The MAC standard specifies the rules by which the TTRT is negotiated by the attached stations.

Asynchronous Services

Initial implementations of FDDI use *asynchronous transmission* to pass data around the ring. Asynchronous transmission is a method of communication in which information is sent when the token holding rules allow transmission. It is designed to use bandwidth not reserved by synchronous services.

NOTE

Asynchronous ring transmission pertains to ring traffic and services that are not extremely delay-sensitive. Do not confuse this asynchronous ring transmission with the asynchronous transmission of data on low-speed lines used by devices such as ASCII terminals.

Synchronous Services

FDDI also specifies *synchronous transmission* services whereby each station is guaranteed a portion of the 100 Mb/s FDDI bandwidth. This percentage is negotiated using a synchronous bandwidth allocation function defined by SMT.

• Logical Link Control

Although Logical Link Control (LLC) is not part of the FDDI standard, FDDI requires LLC for proper ring operation and transmission of user data.

Logical Link Control defines link level services, which allow the transmission of a frame of data between two stations. Figure 27 shows the relationship between LLC and FDDI. FDDI assumes implementation of the IEEE 802.2 LLC standard.

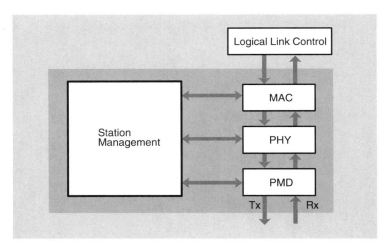

Figure 27 • Relationship between LLC and FDDI

• Frames

Frames are used to transfer information between MAC layers in FDDI. FDDI defines the types of frames, which include:

- MAC frames that carry MAC control data.

- SMT frames that carry FDDI-specific management information between stations.

- LLC frames that carry LLC information.

Like tokens, frames consist of several fields, each containing information that defines a specific frame parameter. Each frame parameter consists of a number of FDDI symbols that define such things as source and destination addresses, information, and a frame-checking sequence for error detection.

MAC Frames

Media Access Control frames include claim frames used in ring initialization and beacon frames used in the process of ring fault isolation.

Because MAC frames are used to initialize the FDDI ring, they do not leave the FDDI network; that is, they do not cross bridges or routers. For example, if a MAC frame from one ring did cross the bridge or router to another ring, it would create confusion for the receiving network.

SMT Frames

Station Management frames carry information that helps control, operate, and maintain the FDDI ring and its member stations.

Because SMT frames are used to control the operation of one FDDI ring only, they do not cross bridges or routers onto the extended LAN. See Chapter 6 for information about SMT frames and how they are used.

LLC Frames

Logical Link Control frames are used to carry information on the FDDI network. LLC frames can be bridged or routed, thus allowing communication between stations on an extended LAN.

• Summary

The Media Access Control protocol is responsible for frame and token construction, sending and receiving frames on the FDDI ring, and delivery of Logical Link Control frames.

The MAC standard defines the timed-token passing method as the means for acquiring access to the ring. To transmit on the ring, a station must first acquire the token. A station holds the token until it has transmitted all of its frames, or until the transmission time for the appropriate service (asynchronous or synchronous) is exhausted.

Frames are the units of transfer between MAC layers in FDDI. MAC and SMT frames carry data and control information for the operation and management of the FDDI network. LLC frames carry user information to stations on the FDDI ring and to the extended LAN. LLC frames can cross bridges and routers onto an extended LAN; MAC and SMT frames cannot.

Chapter 6 • FDDI Technology: SMT Standard

The Station Management (SMT) standard provides the necessary services at the station level to monitor and control an FDDI station. Figure 28 shows how SMT is incorporated into the FDDI architecture. SMT allows stations to work cooperatively within the ring and ensures proper station operation.

FDDI stations can have multiple instances of PMD, PHY, and MAC entities, but only one SMT *entity*.

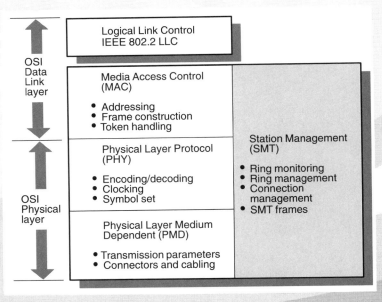

Figure 28 • SMT standard in FDDI

• SMT Components

Station Management contains three major components:

• *Connection Management* (CMT)

• *Ring Management* (RMT)

• SMT frame services

Figure 29 shows how these three SMT components are incorporated into the FDDI architecture.

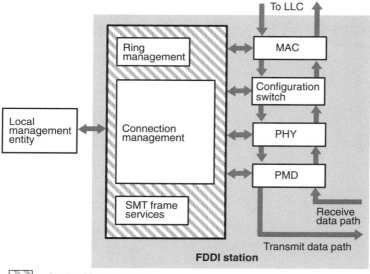

= Station Management

Figure 29 • SMT incorporation into the FDDI architecture

Connection Management

Connection Management (CMT) is the portion of Station Management that performs Physical layer insertion and removal of stations. Remember that FDDI stations can have multiple occurrences of PHYs and MACs. Therefore, one of the functions of CMT is to manage the *configuration switch* (Figure 29) that connects PHYs to MACs and to other PHYs within a station.

Connection Management Functions

Connection Management functions include:

- Connecting a PHY to its neighboring PHY

- Connecting PHYs and MACs via the configuration switch

- Using *trace* diagnostics to identify and isolate a faulty component (see Chapter 7)

Connection Management Components

As shown in Figure 30, CMT contains the following components:

- *Physical Connection Management* (PCM)—Provides for managing the physical connection between adjacent PHYs, including:
  - Establishing the connection
  - Testing the quality of the link before the connection is established (Link Confidence Testing)
  - Continuous monitoring of error rates once the ring is operational (Link Error Monitoring)

- *Configuration Management* (CFM)—Provides for configuring PHY and MAC entities within a station.

- *Entity Coordination Management* (ECM)—Provides for controlling bypass relays, signaling to PCM that the medium is available, and coordination of trace functions.

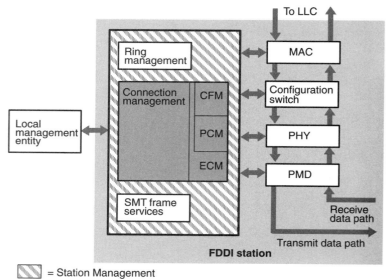

= Station Management

Figure 30 • Connection Management portion of Station Management

Ring Management

The Ring Management (RMT) portion of SMT receives status information from MAC and CMT. Ring Management then reports this status to SMT and higher-level processes. Figure 31 shows RMT in relation to other components of SMT.

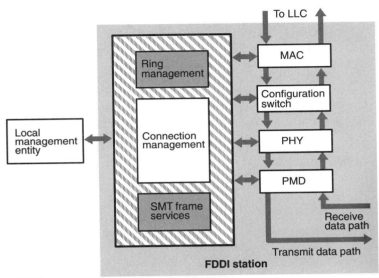

= Station Management

Figure 31 • Ring Management and SMT frame services portion of SMT

Services provided by RMT include:

- Stuck-beacon detection (see Chapter 7). A *beacon* is a specialized frame used by the MAC to announce to other stations that the ring is broken. A *stuck beacon* indicates that a station cannot resolve a ring error condition detected in its receive path.

- Resolution of problems through the trace process (see Chapter 7). Trace provides a recovery mechanism for stuck-beacon conditions on the FDDI ring.

- Determination of a MAC's availability for transmission.

- Detection of duplicate addresses, which will prevent proper operation of the ring even if the ring becomes operational.

SMT Frame Services

The SMT frame services are those portions of SMT that provide the means to control and observe stations on the FDDI network. These services are implemented by different SMT frame classes and types:

- Frame class identifies the function that the frame performs, such as Neighborhood Information Frame (NIF), Status Information Frame (SIF), Parameter Management Frame (PMF), and Status Report Frame (SRF).

- Frame type designates whether the frame is an announcement, request, or response to a request.

Neighborhood Information Frames

Stations determine their upstream and downstream neighbors by exchanging Neighborhood Information Frames (NIFs) as part of the neighbor notification protocol. Stations also use the protocol to determine the existence of duplicate address conditions.

Once upstream neighbor addresses are known to the stations, these addresses can be used to create a logical ring map showing the order in which each station appears in the token path.

Status Information Frames

Stations use Status Information Frames (SIFs) to exchange more detailed information about their characteristics and configuration. In addition, SIFs contain information about the status of each port in a station. The information in SIFs can be used to create a physical ring map that shows the position of each station not only in the token path (logical ring), but in the topology as well.

SIFs are divided into two types: SIF Configuration Frames and SIF Operation Frames. SIF Configuration Frames show the configuration details of a station while SIF Operation Frames show operational detail, such as error rates.

Parameter Management Frames

Parameter Management Frames (PMFs) are used by the Parameter Management Protocol to manage an FDDI station. Management is achieved by operations on the station's *Management Information Base* (MIB) attributes. Operations are performed by an exchange of frames between the manager and the station. Observing an attribute is initiated by a PMF Get Request frame from the management station, followed by a PMF Get Response frame from the target station. Changing a MIB attribute requires a Get Exchange (to check the current value) followed by a PMF Set request/response exchange.

Status Report Frames

Status Report Frames (SRF) are used by the Status Report Protocol to announce station status for use by management stations. SRF frames report conditions and events. Conditions are declared when a station enters certain states, such as "duplicate address detected." Events are instantaneous occurrences, such as the generation of a trace.

• Summary

SMT provides services that monitor and control an FDDI station. The Connection Management portion of SMT is responsible for Physical layer insertion and removal, error monitoring, and the connection of PHYs to MACs within a station.

The Ring Management portion of SMT receives status information and reports this information to SMT and higher-level processes. It detects ring error conditions such as duplicate addresses and stuck-beacon conditions.

The SMT frame services portion of SMT provides control and observation mechanisms for stations on the FDDI network. The various frame types can be used to create logical and physical ring maps, monitor and control MIB variables, and report station conditions and events.

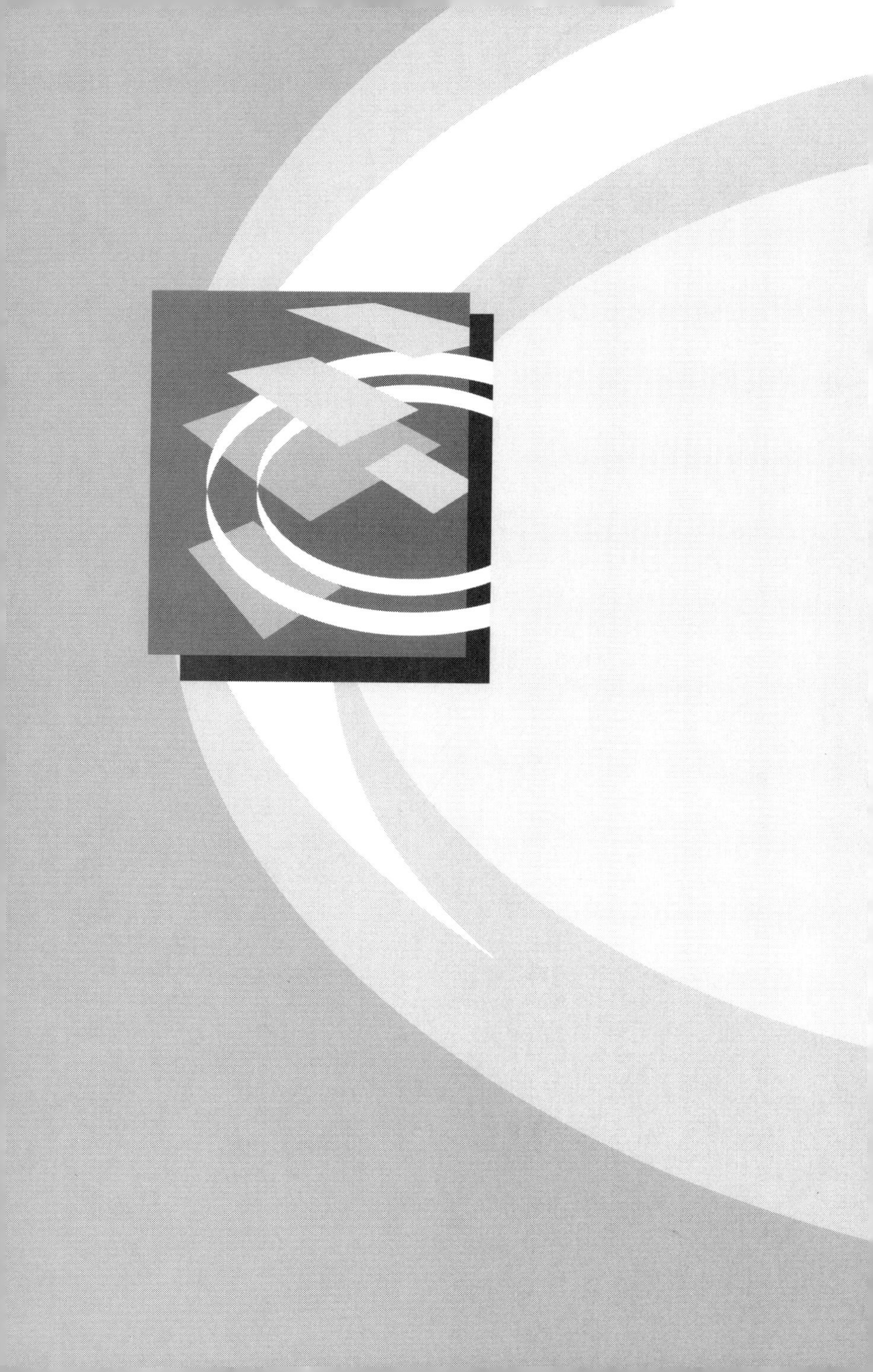

FDDI standards define the functions that control ring operation and maintenance. FDDI technology attempts to circumvent failures to provide continuous ring operation.

After acquiring the token, an active station transmits a frame as a stream of symbols to the next active station on the ring. As each active station receives these symbols, it regenerates and repeats them to the next active device on the ring (its downstream neighbor). When the frame returns to the originating station, it is stripped by that station from the ring.

• Dual Counter-Rotating Ring

The dual *counter-rotating ring* is one of the basic concepts in the FDDI standards. It consists of a primary ring and a secondary ring. The FDDI standards allow both rings to carry data. As shown in Figure 32, the data flows in opposite directions on the two rings. In most cases, particularly in high-bandwidth applications, it is best to use the primary ring for data transmission and the secondary ring as backup. This is especially important when the FDDI ring undergoes its self-healing process during a station or fault condition. In addition, the ability to utilize both rings for data transmission requires stations to include more than one MAC and a bridge/router to join both rings. This adds additional configuration complexity and cost.

FDDI limits total fiber length to 200 kilometers (124 miles). Since the dual-ring topology effectively doubles media length in the event of a fault condition, the actual length of each ring is limited to 100 kilometers (62 miles).

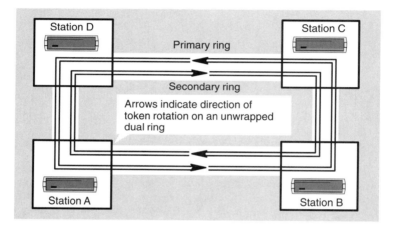

Figure 32 • Counter-rotating ring—conceptual view

Continuing Transmission on the Ring

The dual counter-rotating ring design has the ability to restore ring operation if a device fails or a cable fault occurs. The ring is restored by wrapping the primary ring to the secondary ring to restore the transmission path. This redundancy in the ring design provides a degree of fault tolerance not found in other network standards.

Isolating the Fault

If a cable failure occurs, the stations on each side of the failure reconfigure. They wrap the primary ring to the secondary ring, effectively isolating the fault. This restores continuity to the ring, allowing normal operation to continue. Figure 33 shows this fault isolation technique.

When a wrap occurs, the dual-ring topology changes to a single-ring topology. When the fault is corrected, the topology reverts back to the dual-ring topology. If multiple faults occur, the ring segments into several independent rings.Therefore, when there is more than one fault in the dual ring, communication between all stations is not possible, as there are multiple, disjointed rings.

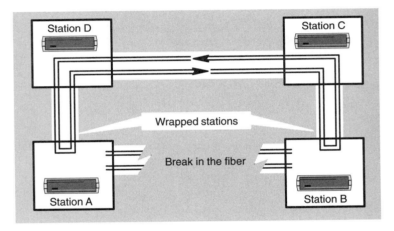

Figure 33 • Counter-rotating ring link fault isolation

If an attached station fails, the devices on each side of the failed station reconfigure to isolate the station from the ring. Figure 34 shows this fault isolation technique.

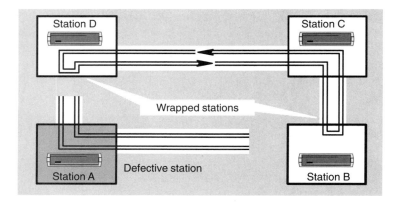

Figure 34 • Counter-rotating ring station fault isolation

In this example, station A is isolated from the ring. The ring remains operational by wrapping the primary and secondary rings at stations B and D. They remain wrapped until the fault is corrected.

• Ring Operation

FDDI ring operation includes connection establishment, ring initialization, steady-state operation, and ring maintenance. Timers are used to regulate these operations.

Timers

Each station on the FDDI ring uses three timers to regulate its operation. These timers are administered locally by the individual stations:

- The *token rotation timer* (TRT)

- The *token holding timer* (THT)

- The *valid transmission timer* (TVX)

Token Rotation Timer

TRT is used to time the duration of operations in a station. This timer is critical to the successful operation of the FDDI network. This timer controls ring scheduling during normal operation and fault recovery times when the ring is not operational.

TRT is initialized to different values depending on the state of the ring. During steady-state operation, TRT expires when the target token rotation time (TTRT) has been exceeded. Stations negotiate the value for TTRT via the *claim process*.

Token Holding Timer

THT controls the length of time that a station can initiate asynchronous frames. A station holding the token can begin asynchronous transmissions if THT has not expired. THT is initialized with the value corresponding to the difference between the arrival of the token and TTRT.

Valid Transmission Timer

TVX times the period between valid transmissions on the ring. TVX detects excessive ring noise, token loss, and other faults. When the station receives a valid frame or token, the valid transmission timer resets. If TVX expires, then the station will start a ring initialization sequence to restore the ring to proper operation.

• Connection Establishment

In order for the ring to form, stations must establish connections with their neighbors. The CMT portion of SMT controls this physical connection process. At power up or on a connection restart, stations recognize their neighbors by transmitting and acknowledging defined line state sequences (as defined in Chapter 4). See Figure 35.

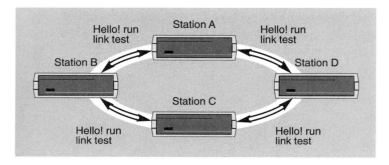

Figure 35 • Ring power up

In order to establish a link, stations:

1. Exchange information on port type and connection rules.

2. Negotiate the length of the link confidence test, which checks the quality of the links between stations.

3. Run the link confidence test for the negotiated time.

4. Exchange results.

If the connection type is accepted, and the link confidence test passes, the stations complete the physical connection by transmitting another defined line state sequence. This process is repeated for each link in the dual ring. Eventually all stations join the ring.

• Ring Initialization

After the stations establish the connection, FDDI requires the stations to bid for the right to initialize the ring (i.e. generate a token) by negotiating a target token rotation time. This ensures that stations receive guaranteed service time. The TTRT can be set based on the:

• Number of attached stations

• Length of the ring

• Time required by each station to transmit data over the ring

• Balance of low latency and adequate bandwidth

During ring initialization, stations negotiate the TTRT with other stations to determine which station will issue the token. This process of negotiation is called the claim process.

Claim Process

The claim process determines which station initializes the ring. The process is similar to an auction. In an auction, the highest bid wins (claims) the item. During ring initialization, the station with the lowest bid (in time) for the TTRT wins the right to initialize the ring.

The claim process begins when the Media Access Control entity in one or more stations enters the claim state. In this state, the MAC in each station continually transmits claim frames. A claim frame contains the station's address and bid for the TTRT. Stations in the ring compare the incoming claim frames with their own bid for target token rotation time. If the frame has a:

• Shorter time bid, the station repeats the claim frame and stops sending its own claim.

• Longer time bid, the station removes the claim frame and continues sending frames with its own bid for TTRT.

When a station receives its own claim frame, that station wins the right to initialize the ring. If two or more stations make identical bids, the station with the longest and highest address wins the bidding.

The winning station initializes the ring by issuing a token. This token passes around the ring without being captured by any station. Instead, as each station receives the token, it sets its own TTRT to match the TTRT of the winning station. On the second token rotation, stations may send synchronous traffic. On the token's third rotation, stations can begin transmitting asynchronous data.

Example of the Claim Process

Figure 36 is used to illustrate how the stations negotiate (or bid) for the right to initialize the ring. In this example, stations A and C are issuing shorter bids than stations B and D. Station C is issuing a shorter bid than station A.

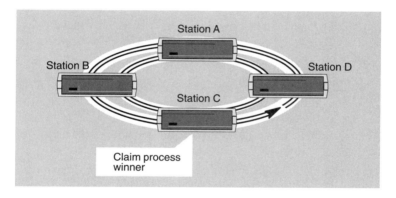

Figure 36 • Stations negotiating for the right to initialize the ring

The process of negotiation is as follows:

1. All active stations start issuing claim frames.

2. Station D receives a shorter claim from station C, stops sending its own claim, and repeats station C's shorter claim to station A. Meanwhile:

   – Station B receives a shorter claim from station A, stops sending its own claim, and repeats station A's shorter claim to station C.

– Station C receives station A's claim frame but continues sending its own shorter claim frame.

3. Station A receives station C's shorter claim from station D, stops sending its own claim, and repeats station C's shorter claim to station B.

4. Station B receives station C's shorter claim from station A and repeats station C's shorter claim to station C.

5. Station C receives its own claim from station B. Station C sets the TTRT and issues a token to initialize the ring.

This negotiating process supports fair access to the ring at the frame level.

• Steady-State Operation

Once the ring is initialized, steady-state operation can begin. When in the steady state, stations exchange frames using the timed-token protocol. The ring remains in the steady state until a new claim process is initiated; for example, when a new station joins the ring.

Asynchronous and Synchronous Services

Two types of services are provided by FDDI—asynchronous and synchronous. Asynchronous services are designed for bandwidth insensitive applications such as datagram traffic. Asynchronous frames are designed to be transmitted during the time when the station does not require the bandwidth that synchronous service guarantees.

Synchronous frames are sent at any time as long as the bandwidth negotiated via the synchronous bandwidth allocation is not exceeded. This service is useful for frames that must have guaranteed delivery within a time period of 2xTTRT. Such frames include compressed audio and video, among other things.

Timed-Token Protocol

The timed-token protocol includes a number of steps by which a station acquires the right to begin transmission. Figure 37 shows an overview of frame transmission using the FDDI timed-token protocol.

When an FDDI station wants to transmit a frame it:

1. Waits until it detects the token.

2. Captures the token.

3. Stops the token repeat process. (Since there is no token on the ring, this action prevents other stations from transmitting data onto the ring.)

4. Begins sending frames. (Frames can be sent until there is no more data to send, and/or the token holding rules require surrender of the token.)

5. Releases the token onto the ring for use by another station.

All active stations, except the sending station on an FDDI network, receive and repeat each frame. Each station compares the destination address of each frame with its own, and checks for frame errors.

If the addresses match, the receiving station copies the frame and sets status symbols (control indicators) to show that the station has recognized its address and copied the frame.

Repeating stations check for errors and re-transmit the frames to the next station. If the station detects an error, it sets an error indicator.

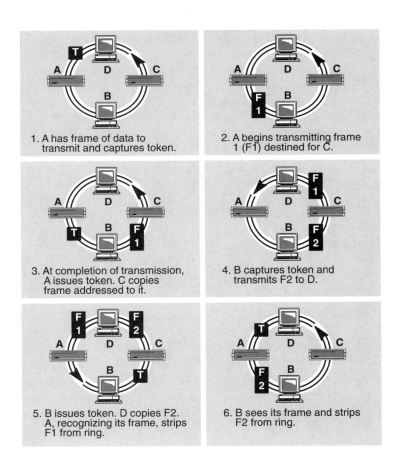

1. A has frame of data to transmit and captures token.

2. A begins transmitting frame 1 (F1) destined for C.

3. At completion of transmission, A issues token. C copies frame addressed to it.

4. B captures token and transmits F2 to D.

5. B issues token. D copies F2. A, recognizing its frame, strips F1 from ring.

6. B sees its frame and strips F2 from ring.

Figure 37 • Overview of frame transmission

After the frame circles the ring, the station that sent it removes (strips) it from the ring. Stripping causes partial frames, called *fragments,* to be left on the ring.

Frame Fragments

To minimize delay, the station reads and repeats the frame fields immediately as it receives the frame. The first part of a frame contains frame class information followed by destination address, source address, and data. When the sending station receives a frame and recognizes its own source address, it removes (strips) the remainder of the frame from the ring. The first part of the frame has already been repeated (creating a frame fragment) and is on the ring.

Each FDDI station makes sure that frame fragments do not degrade ring operation. The fragments are removed either by a transmitter or by operations of the repeat filter of each station's PHY.

Scrubbing

The ring reconfigures when attached devices enter or leave the ring. During this process, stray frames can be introduced to the new topology. These stray frames were generated by a device that is no longer part of the new topology. They can no longer be identified as belonging to any particular attached device.

To remove these strays, a station sends a series of idle symbols to the ring. At the same time, MAC strips the ring of frames and tokens. After this is done, the active stations enter the claim process.

The time taken to scrub the ring guarantees that all frames on the ring have been created after the reconfiguration occurred. This prevents old frames from continually circulating on the ring.

• Ring Maintenance

The responsibility for monitoring ring integrity is distributed among all stations on the ring. Each station monitors the ring for conditions that require ring initialization including:

- Ring inactivity longer than the valid transmission time

- A physical or logical break in the ring

Valid Transmission Timer

Stations use TVX to detect a break in ring activity. The valid transmission timer times the duration between receptions. If this interval exceeds the value set in the timer, an error condition is indicated. Stations then enter the claim process. If the claim process fails to generate a token, the stations enter the beacon process.

Beacon Process

A beacon is a specialized frame used by the MAC to announce to other stations that the ring is broken. Think of a beacon frame as saying, "I've found a problem." The station generating the beacon waits to hear its own frame as an indicator that the problem is corrected.

An FDDI station can start the beacon process when the claim process fails or if station management requests it. When this happens, the station begins continuous transmission of beacon frames.

The MAC uses beacon frames to announce that the ring is broken and to locate and isolate the fault, if possible. If a station receives:

- A beacon from its upstream neighbor, it repeats that beacon and stops its own.

- Its own beacon, it assumes the logical ring is restored, stops beaconing, and begins the claim process.

- No beacon, it transmits a continuous beacon stream.

Stuck-Beacon Condition

A stuck-beacon timer under the control of the Ring Management component of SMT measures the duration of the beacon transmission. If beaconing exceeds the timer limit (approximately 10 seconds), Ring Management begins stuck-beacon recovery procedures, which attempt to restore the ring to normal operation.

The recovery procedure begins with the transmission of a special frame called a directed beacon. A directed beacon informs the ring of the stuck condition. If the ring has not recovered by the end of this transmission, then Ring Management initiates the trace function.

Trace Function

The trace function uses PHY signaling (i.e., line states) to recover from a stuck-beacon condition. The fault is localized to the beaconing MAC and its nearest upstream neighbor. Figure 38 shows the trace sequence of events.

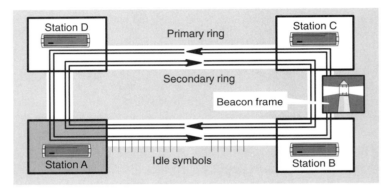

Figure 38 • Detection of defective station using the trace function

In this figure, defective station A transmits continuous idle symbols. Downstream station B times out TVX, sends claims, and then fails the claim process since station A failed to repeat the claim frames. It then enters the beacon process.

After approximately 10 seconds, station B detects that it is stuck beaconing and sends a trace message to station A on the secondary ring using Physical layer signaling. The receipt of the trace message causes stations A and B to leave the ring and perform a self-test. If the fault is in station A, it remains down, and station B rejoins the ring. If the self-test "fixes" station A, it too will rejoin the ring.

• Summary

One of the basic concepts in the FDDI standards is the dual counter-rotating ring, which consists of a primary ring and a secondary ring. The data flows in opposite directions on the rings.

Stations form the ring by establishing connections. Connection rules guarantee that the ring will be properly formed to enhance reliability.

The dual counter-rotating ring design restores ring operation if a device on either ring fails or a fiber fault occurs. The ring is restored by wrapping the primary ring to the secondary ring to restore the transmission path. This redundancy in ring design provides a degree of fault tolerance not found in other network standards. If both rings are used to carry data, the aggregate bandwidth is limited to 100 Mb/s during the period when the ring wraps.

Timers regulate activity on the ring. For example, the token rotation timer times the receipt of tokens. This time is initialized to a given value depending on the target token rotation time established by negotiation between active stations on the ring. Stations bid for the right to set the TTRT, initialize the ring, and start circulating the token.

To transmit, a station captures the token, stops the repeat process, and sends asynchronous or synchronous frames until none is left to send or the appropriate timer expires. Then the station releases the token onto the ring for use by another station.

A transmitting station is responsible for removing (stripping) all frames that it sends. This process leaves frame fragments on the ring that are removed by the next transmitting station or by the cumulative action of repeat filters in many stations.

Stray frames and frame fragments that may be left on the ring by a station leaving the ring are removed by a scrubbing function. This function prevents old frames from continually circulating on the ring.

Beaconing and tracing are two important mechanisms provided for fault recovery. They are designed to correct serious breaks in the ring continuity.

Chapter 8 • The Network: Structured Cabling

Physically, networks consist of active and passive devices and the cable that connects them. Structured cabling defines a wiring system and its components. It provides a comprehensive approach to the framework for physical and logical connections on the network.

A universal structured cabling infrastructure allows access to any information technology and is independent of the equipment it serves. It allows network managers and planners to make changes easily and with minimal disruption to the organization.

• FDDI and Structured Cabling

The need to have FDDI integral to structured cabling is a result of:

- Increasing numbers of users spread over large geographic areas

- More powerful computers that apply large network loads

- Acceptance of client/server systems and computer-intensive applications such as imaging, graphics, and video conferencing

A structured cabling system, which is independent of application, is a good integration path for FDDI. This allows connection of the campus backbone and interdepartmental FDDI backbones to current interdepartmental and departmental LANs.

● Topology Criteria

Network topology is the physical arrangement of the structured cabling and components that connect a site's buildings and floors. Several factors determine the topology:

● The size of the network, including the number of nodes

● The frequency, volume, and type of communication between nodes

● How often nodes are added, changed, or removed from the network

● The bandwidth, level of fault tolerance, and redundant paths needed to support the network and provide for future growth

All of these factors determine the topology best suited for a particular installation.

● EIA/TIA Standard for Structured Cabling

The Electronic Industries Association/Telecommunications Industries Association (EIA/TIA) 568 standard for commercial building wiring covers four general areas:

● The media (fiber-optic cable, coaxial cable, twisted-pair cable)

● Topology of the media

● Terminations and connectors

● Administration

Building wiring systems defined by the standard are designed to have a useful life in excess of 10 years. The EIA/TIA 568 standard specifies the backbone and horizontal media, as well as the administration component, topology, and distance.

Structured cable plants have distinct advantages over unstructured solutions as detailed in Table 2.

Table 2 • Comparison of structured and unstructured cabling

Structured Cabling	Unstructured Cabling
Application independent	Usually application dependent
People and equipment moved easily without rewiring	Often requires rewiring
Anticipates growth and change	Does not easily allow for growth and change
Flexible, modular design	Nonflexible, nonmodular design
Easily managed and maintained; problem isolation is easy	Limited management and problem isolation capabilities

Hierarchical Physical Star Topology

The EIA/TIA 568 standard employs a hierarchical physical star topology. Any logical topology such as point-to-point, ring, tree, and dual ring of trees easily maps into this star topology. The advantages include:

• Easy configuration supporting a wide range of active equipment

• Provision of centralized points for managing and maintaining the network

• A platform for modular and nondisruptive growth of the network

• Topology Subsystems

The EIA/TIA 568 standard divides wiring topology into the subsystems shown in Figure 39.

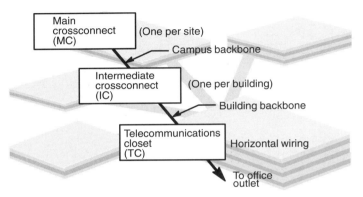

Figure 39 • Wiring topology subsystems

The subsystems are as follows:

• Campus backbone subsystem with its *main crossconnect* (MC)

• Building backbone subsystem with its *intermediate crossconnect* (IC)

• Horizontal subsystem with its *telecommunications closet* (TC)

• Work area wiring subsystem

• Administration subsystem

Campus Backbone Subsystem

The *campus backbone subsystem* links clusters of buildings together within a site. One of the buildings contains the main crossconnect in an equipment room.

The MC consists of active and passive components that provide the backbone for the buildings on the site. Fiber-optic cable and other media are installed between buildings either above ground or in underground conduits (Figure 40).

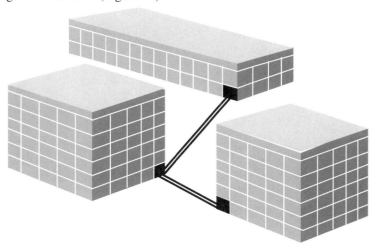

Figure 40 • Campus backbone subsystem

Building Backbone Subsystem

The *building backbone subsystem* (also called a riser) provides the link between the campus backbone and the horizontal/workgroup areas (Figure 41).

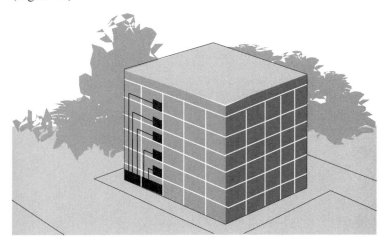

Figure 41 • Building backbone subsystem

This subsystem consists of one intermediate crossconnect (IC) located in an equipment room. The IC contains active and passive components that connect the building backbone cabling to the campus backbone cabling. Fiber-optic cable is installed from the IC to telecommunications closets on each floor.

Horizontal Subsystem

The horizontal subsystem provides the connection from the building backbone to the work area wiring. The TC provides the site for this connection, and consists of passive and active components. If the configuration on the floor does not require fiber-optic cabling, the fiber ends in the TC. If current or future applications warrant it, fiber-optic cable can be extended from the TC to the office. Adding connectors to the fiber-optic cable can be done on an as-needed basis.

Work Area Wiring Subsystem

The work area wiring subsystem connects the active devices (such as an FDDI workstation) to the telecommunications closet. This subsystem frequently consists of a communication box called a telecommunications outlet that can be configured to accept various cable connections for data, voice, image, and video.

Administration Subsystem

The administration subsystem consists of the hardware and documentation for linking and managing the other subsystems. It provides the *crossconnects*, *interconnects*, and labeling needed to maintain the end-to-end connectivity of the network.

Crossconnect means that two cables from the same or different subsystem connect at a patch panel. Crossconnects use panel-mounted couplers and a patch cable.

Interconnects join two cables with a single pair of connectors. FDDI uses either a panel-mounted fiber-optic coupler or a wallbox-mounted fiber-optic coupler. For example, the fiber-optic wallbox in the user's work area is the interconnect point for the FDDI workstation and the FDDI network.

Figure 42 illustrates the structured wiring subsystems.

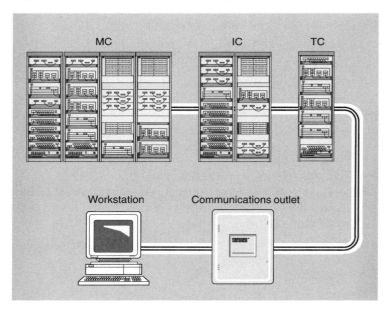

Figure 42 • EIA/TIA 568 structured wiring subsystems

• Planning for a Structured Network

A structured infrastructure is an ideal platform for high-speed FDDI networks. There are three phases in planning for and implementing a structured wiring system.

- During the preplanning phase, a network analysis and site survey should be done to determine the space, safety, and grounding requirements.

- During the cable plant design phase, concrete concept diagrams should be created, as well as detailed diagrams for cable runs in the buildings.

- During the installation and certification phase, procedures should be performed to make sure that the cable plant meets standards, specifications, and quality for top network performance.

• Summary

A universal, application-independent, structured wiring system is a good integration path for any network. Such a system permits the connection of the campus backbone and interdepartmental FDDI backbones to current interdepartmental and departmental LANs.

The EIA/TIA 568 standard for commercial building wiring defines the:

- Campus backbone subsystem with its main crossconnect

- Intermediate backbone subsystem with its intermediate crossconnect

- Horizontal subsystem with its telecommunications closet

In addition, the standard defines structured wiring for the work area and the administrative subsystem. Implementation of an FDDI network can be accomplished more easily with a standards-based wiring system.

Chapter 9 • The FDDI Network: Topology

An FDDI network consists of physical and logical topologies that can be configured in a variety of ways.

• Physical and Logical Topologies

All networks have physical and logical topologies.

- The *physical topology* refers to the actual arrangement of the cables and hardware that make up the network.

- The *logical topology* refers to the actual path a frame follows from its source to its destination. The path of the logical topology varies, depending on traffic flow and the number and location of active stations on the network.

• Typical FDDI Configurations

FDDI networks can be organized in various ways. A network configuration with only dual attachment stations results in a logical and physical ring. FDDI allows for more versatility than this one configuration. For example, when concentrators are added to the network, a branching tree topology develops.

FDDI is likely to be implemented in three ways:

- As a high-speed backbone connecting mid-speed LANs, such as those found in IEEE 802.3 and IEEE 802.5 applications

- As a high-speed workgroup LAN connecting workstations or servers

- As a high-speed connection between host computers or host computers-to-peripheral equipment, such as those found in a data center

• FDDI Topologies

The FDDI standards permit a number of topologies. The following four topologies are of particular importance:

- Standalone concentrator with attached stations

- Dual ring

- Tree of concentrators

- Dual ring of trees

Standalone Concentrator

The standalone concentrator topology consists of a single concentrator and its attached stations (Figure 43). These stations can be either Single Attachment Station (SAS) or Dual Attachment Station (DAS) devices. For example, the concentrator can connect multiple high-performance devices in a workgroup.

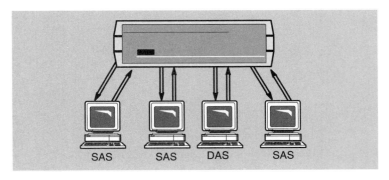

Figure 43 • Standalone concentrator topology

Figure 43 shows an independent workgroup topology that can use existing structured wiring, affording significant cost savings in prewired sites. The logical ring is formed by the stations and the concentrator, with the token path illustrated by the direction of the arrows.

Dual Ring

The dual-ring topology consists of dual attachment stations connected directly to the dual ring. This topology is useful when there are a limited number of stations (Figure 44). A dual ring of DAS devices, however, does not easily lend itself to additions, moves, and changes.

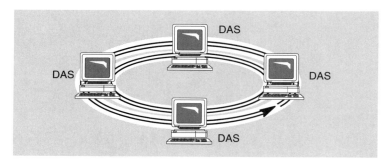

Figure 44 • Dual ring

Because each station is part of the backbone wiring, the behavior of each user is critical to the operation of the ring. The simple act of a user disconnecting a dual attachment workstation causes a break in the ring.

In the event of a single failure, a dual ring self-heals by wrapping the primary and secondary rings. However, multiple failures result in two or more segmented rings. Each ring is fully functional, but there is no access to the other rings. For this reason, dual rings should only be implemented when there is little risk of users disturbing the network connection.

Tree of Concentrators

The tree of concentrators is the preferred choice when wiring together large groups of user devices. Concentrators are wired in a hierarchical star topology with one concentrator serving as the root of the tree.

In this configuration, one FDDI concentrator is designated as the root (Figure 45). Cables run from this concentrator to single attachment stations, dual attachment stations, or other concentrators. This topology provides greater flexibility for adding and removing FDDI concentrators and stations, or changing their location without disrupting the FDDI LAN.

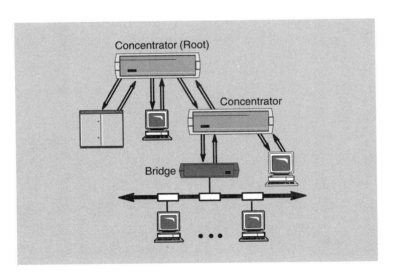

Figure 45 • Tree of concentrators wired in a hierarchical star configuration

Additional concentrators can connect to the second tier of concentrators, as needed, to support new users. The tree configuration may connect:

• All stations in a single building

• A large number of stations on one floor of a building

The tree topology is well suited to structured cabling systems.

Tree topologies also allow network managers to better control access of end-user systems to the network. Inoperative systems can be easily removed from the network by the concentrator. Also, the network manager can remotely access the concentrator to bypass a station.

Dual Ring of Trees

The fourth topology described in the FDDI standards is the *dual ring of trees*. In this topology, concentrators cascade from other concentrators connected to a dual ring (Figure 46). This places the dual ring where it is needed most—in the backbone.

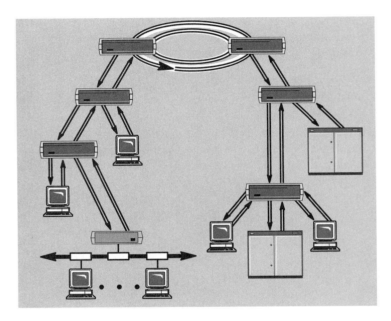

Figure 46 • Use of concentrators in the dual ring of trees topology

Most Flexible Topology

The dual ring of trees is the recommended topology for FDDI. It provides a high degree of fault tolerance and increases the availability of the backbone ring.

The dual ring of trees is also the most flexible topology. The tree branches out by simply adding concentrators that connect to the ring through upper-level concentrators attached to the dual ring. Tree branches can be extended as long as the station number or ring distance limits are not exceeded.

Stations attached to concentrators connected to the dual ring or configured in tree topologies can be removed from the FDDI LAN as needed. Concentrators can easily bypass inactive or defective stations without disrupting the overall network.

Guaranteed Backup Data Path

The dual ring at the backbone guarantees a backup data path to all concentrators and dual attachment stations in the dual ring.

Figure 47 shows potential points of failure on a single ring. This problem is inherent in a single-ring design. In large installations where the probability of ring or station failure is high, this type of disruption is unacceptable.

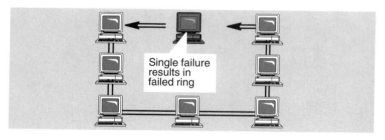

Figure 47 • Potential points of failure in a single ring

As discussed in Chapter 7, the dual counter-rotating ring design of FDDI eliminates most problems associated with the single-ring design, although it only corrects a single failure on the dual ring.

Figure 48 shows what happens when a ring of DAS devices is subject to multiple ring failures or disconnects. The result is two or more segmented rings with no access to the other rings. These failures can be caused by the simple act of a user turning off a workstation.

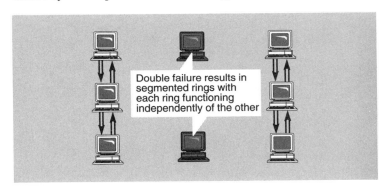

Figure 48 • Failure of two stations in a dual ring causes segmented rings

How the Dual Ring of Trees Solves the Problem

Using FDDI concentrators configured in a dual ring of trees can solve the segmented ring problem. The dual ring of trees topology creates a large, sophisticated network that sustains the loss of all stations connected to the concentrators without losing ring integrity. In this topology, concentrators electronically bypass ring disruptions.

Figure 49 shows two concentrators attached to the dual ring with two bypassed stations. Connection Management provides for the removal of defective links with no disruption of service to remaining stations.

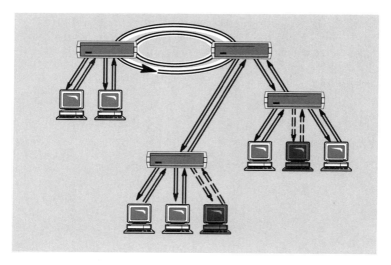

Figure 49 • *Concentrators give continuous service to a dual ring of trees*

The dual ring of trees topology proves to be a more dynamic and reliable solution to topology problems than either the single or dual-ring approaches. With the dual ring of trees, the best of both topologies (dual ring and tree of concentrators) is available to network users.

Dual Homing, an FDDI Redundant Topology

The FDDI connection rules allow for several redundant topologies. A redundant topology provides several logical paths for connecting to the network. The FDDI standards allow redundant paths in tree topologies as well as in the dual ring. This redundancy is provided by a mechanism known as *dual homing.*

Figure 50 shows an example of dual homing. Concentrators X and Y are connected to the dual ring. Concentrator Z is typically attached to the ring through the primary connection to Concentrator Y. If this connection fails, the backup link is automatically activated, thus maintaining service to the stations attached to Concentrator Z.

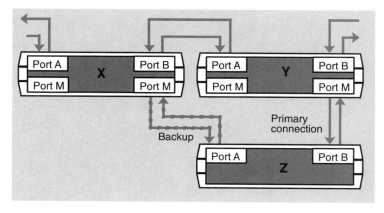

Figure 50 • Dual homing in a dual ring of trees topology

Redundant topologies are useful in cases where there may be a station or cable failure. They are used in installations where network uptime is critical, as in banking or finance. Note that any DAS or concentrator can be dual homed. Thus, if an individual station must have redundancy, its A and B ports can be connected to different concentrators, like concentrator Z is connected to concentrators X and Y in Figure 50.

• Application Scenarios

Following are examples of typical FDDI network applications.

The FDDI Workgroup LAN

The FDDI workgroup LAN allows a group of users to function as one unit (Figure 51).

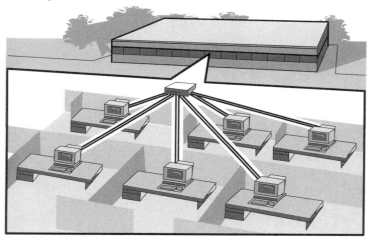

Figure 51 • *FDDI workgroup LAN*

When the LAN requires high bandwidth and fault recovery features, end-user devices can be installed as:

- Dedicated FDDI workgroups consisting of a concentrator and single attachment or dual attachment stations

- Dual attachment stations connected in a dual ring configuration for a limited number of users

For most applications, the workstations are connected to a concentrator. This concentrator can be standalone, or one of many in a dual ring of trees configuration.

The FDDI Interdepartmental Network

The FDDI interdepartmental network links various departmental LANs within a building. It can connect them to the building data center and also to the larger campus network. The best topology for an interdepartmental LAN is a tree configuration (Figure 52).

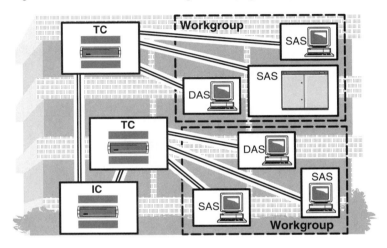

Figure 52 • Interdepartmental FDDI network configured as a tree

The central concentrator located at the IC connects the building LAN to the larger campus network. In small organizations that are not spread over several buildings, the interdepartmental network can be the corporate backbone LAN.

The FDDI Campus Network

The FDDI campus network can assume three topologies: a dual ring, a tree, or a dual ring of trees.

Figure 53 shows an FDDI campus network installed in a dual ring of trees topology. In this example, the concentrators in buildings A, B, and C form the ring portion of the dual ring of trees.

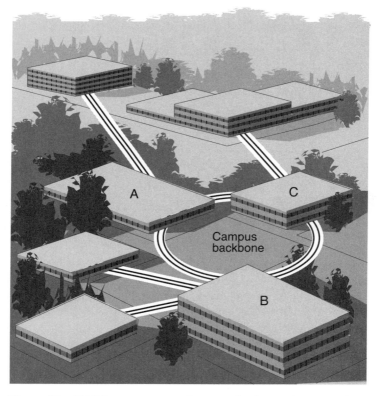

Figure 53 • FDDI campus network using a dual ring of trees topology

In the dual ring of trees topology, concentrators, bridges, and routers are installed in a dual ring with cables radiating outward to concentrators or bridges in other buildings. This topology:

- Provides administration points for maintenance, service, and fault isolation

- Is easier to add to, move, or reconfigure within individual buildings

• Summary

The power and versatility of an FDDI network allows it to be configured in many ways: as a high-speed backbone, a high-speed workgroup, and host-to-host/host-to-peripheral configurations..

FDDI networks offer four typical configurations: standalone, dual ring, tree of concentrators, and dual ring of trees.

Small workgroups can be configured in either standalone concentrator or dual ring topologies. When wiring large groups of user devices together, however, the preferred choice is either a tree of concentrators or a dual ring of trees.

The recommended choice is the dual ring of trees because it offers extensive flexibility as well as redundancy. Another advantage of the dual ring of trees is that it yields a more manageable network. The tree branches out, as required, by adding concentrators.

Dual homing, a redundant tree topology, provides protection where network uptime is critical. A tree of concentrators and a dual ring of trees can dual home one or more concentrators or stations.

FDDI topologies can be configured as workgroups, interdepartmental LANs, and as the campus backbone.

Chapter 10 • FDDI Components: Concentrators

The FDDI concentrator (Figure 54) plays a central role in the topologies used in FDDI. It offers the flexibility necessary to accommodate the diverse wiring schemes found in different sites. It is a key component in the dual ring of trees topology, providing a connection point for end-stations and other FDDI devices in a dual ring of trees.

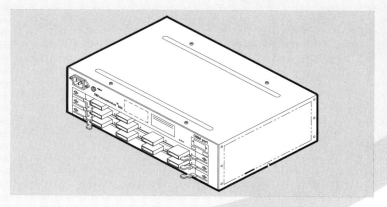

Figure 54 • The FDDI concentrator

● What the Concentrator Offers

The FDDI concentrator is a Physical layer repeater that allows the attachment of multiple single attachment stations, dual attachment stations, or other concentrators to the FDDI network. By cascading concentrators, network implementors can create a dual ring of trees topology. When used in a standalone configuration, the concentrator becomes the hub in a workgroup topology.

The concentrator can be designed as either a Dual Attachment Concentrator (DAC) or Single Attachment Concentrator (SAC). Figure 55 shows the dual ring of trees using both single attachment concentrators and dual attachment concentrators. Both types act as connection points to the FDDI network and enable station connections to the ring via M ports. The DAC allows connection of its M ports to either the primary or secondary ring. The SAC connects to either ring as determined by the upper level concentrator.

The DAC connects to the dual ring via its A and B ports. The SAC, however, does not connect directly to the dual ring; it accesses the ring via its S port, which connects to an M port of another concentrator. Note, however, that a DAC can also be used wherever a single attachment concentrator is used.

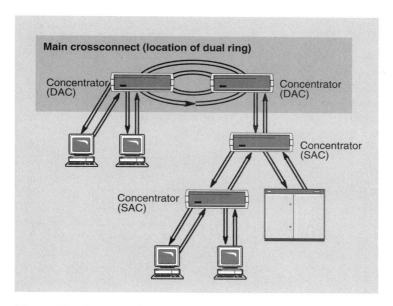

Figure 55 • Using single attachment concentrators and dual attachment concentrators in a dual ring of trees

Concentrators With and Without Media Access Control

FDDI standards specify that concentrators can be created with or without MAC entities. MAC provides services to the concentrator that are required for remote stations to manage a concentrator.

Concentrators without MAC entities are used mostly in small, standalone topologies within limited geographical areas. In these cases, network management services may be an unnecessary expense. A lower cost alternative is device-specific out-of-band management that may not require a MAC.

Concentrator Architecture

In addition to the A, B, or S ports that connect it to the ring, the concentrator includes an SMT entity, a configuration switch, and a number of M ports (see Figure 56). M ports establish connections with A, B, or S ports of other stations, under the control of SMT. Once a connection is established, the configuration switch is toggled, and the port is allowed into the ring. If a problem is detected, the configuration switch isolates the problem port from the ring.

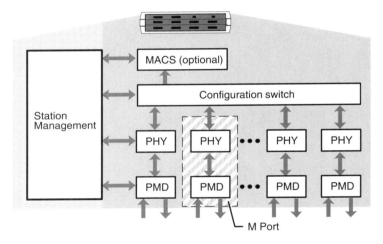

Figure 56 • Basic structure of the concentrator

Concentrator Functions

The concentrator performs two important functions electronically: port (and thus station) bypass and port (station) insertion. The concentrator's internal configuration switch performs these functions. The internal configuration switch allows ports into and out of the ring either by:

- Control of the FDDI Connection Management protocols

- A user-issued command from a management station

Bypass

Ports are automatically bypassed in response to detected faults or management requests. The bypass capabilities of the concentrator enable it to logically disconnect an attached station from the ring if:

- The concentrator detects a high error rate or a defective connection.

- A network management entity requests the concentrator to remove the port.

- A user disconnects a cable or powers down the station.

Notice that the bypass function of the concentrator enhances the reliability of the FDDI ring beyond that possible with a DAS-only architecture. No matter how many ports are bypassed, the remainder of the network remains fully operational. Services are denied only to those stations attached to the bypassed ports.

It is important to note that the bypass feature of a concentrator is not limited in the same way as an Optical Bypass Relay (OBR) is limited. The concentrator allows any number of ports to be bypassed, up to the 500 station limit of the FDDI architecture.

Insertion

Once the port makes a connection to its attached station, the concentrator inserts the station into either the primary or secondary ring. The concentrator opens the configuration switch, scrubs the ring, and connects the port into the ring. This process takes a very short time (about 14 milliseconds for a fully configured FDDI ring).

Network Management

Optional network management software allows the user to configure a concentrator to the needs of the network. This software allows the network manager to monitor the health of the concentrator, determine what stations are attached to which ports, or remove/insert stations from the concentrator. Concentrators can be managed via SMT frame services, the SNMP protocol, or a vendor proprietary protocol.

• Summary

The FDDI concentrator is a key component in the dual ring of trees topology, providing a connection point for end-stations or other FDDI devices. The concentrator is an active device that actually controls the topology of the network. The dual attachment concentrator has A and B ports for connection to the dual ring. The single attachment concentrator connects to the ring via an M port in another concentrator.

Concentrators can be built with or without a MAC entity. However, remote network management of a concentrator cannot be performed without MAC.

In addition to acting as the connection point to the FDDI LAN for SAS or DAS devices, the concentrator allows stations to be inserted and removed with minimal effect on the operation of the ring. This is automatically done by the concentrator or by a command from a management station.

FDDI standards define two station types: Single Attachment Station (SAS) and Dual Attachment Station (DAS). High-performance workstations, LAN interconnect devices such as bridges, and other computer equipment connect to FDDI through one of these two methods.

• The FDDI Connection

The *physical connection* shown in Figure 57 is basic to the FDDI ring design. It is through this connection that attached devices pass information over the ring.

An FDDI physical connection is formed between the Physical layers (PHY/PMD) of two stations connected by a cable. FDDI requires that all connections in the ring be point-to-point and bidirectional. Each attachment to the network has a transmit and receive component. A physical connection contains two fibers which connect the transmitters and receivers of adjacent stations. A SAS has provision for one physical connection while a DAS has two physical connections.

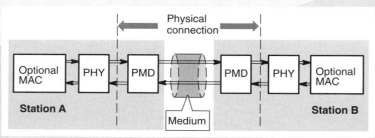

Figure 57 • FDDI physical connection

• Single Attachment Station

The simplest means of connection to the FDDI ring is the SAS (Figure 58). The SAS has one S-type port and connects to the ring via the M port of a concentrator.

The SAS, shown in Figure 58, consists of a single instance of MAC, SMT, PHY, and PMD. In the dual ring of trees topology, the SAS proves to be a reliable, cost-effective method for connecting to the FDDI network.

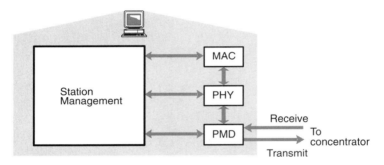

Figure 58 • Single attachment station architecture

To prevent a defective SAS device from disrupting the ring, fault control is provided by the concentrator. Design features in the concentrator allow it to detect problems in the connection caused by a failed SAS, and to isolate the failing SAS from the ring.

• Dual Attachment Station

The DAS connects to both the primary and secondary rings of the FDDI dual ring. The DAS consists of two PHYs, two PMDs, one or (optionally) two MACs, a single instance of SMT, and an optional optical bypass relay. A DAS has two ports: A and B. The A port connects to another station's B port while the B port connects to another station's A port. Figure 59 is a conceptual view of a DAS.

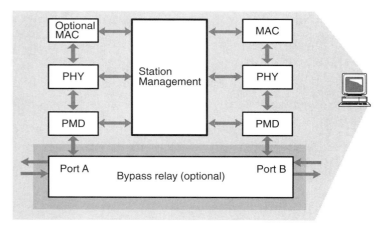

Figure 59 • Dual attachment station architecture

The DAS does not require the use of a concentrator to connect to the FDDI ring. Because it can access both FDDI rings, the DAS is capable of wrapping the ring in case of a device failure.

A DAS-only FDDI network, however, has its limitations. For example, when two or more DAS stations fail or are disconnected, the FDDI LAN can be segmented into disparate networks thus isolating users from the resources on the LAN.

Like SAS devices, DAS devices can also be connected into concentrator tree structures by connecting the B port to the concentrator. The benefits of using a concentrator are twofold:

- Isolates the DAS from the ring by electronically bypassing the DAS if it fails or is disconnected

- Provides redundancy via dual homing by connecting each port of the DAS to two separate concentrators that are attached to the ring

While the FDDI standards support DAS stations connected directly to the dual ring, the use of SAS or DAS end-user stations configured with a concentrator in a dual ring of trees is a more manageable and reliable FDDI implementation.

• FDDI Controllers

FDDI *controllers* connect end-user stations or systems to the FDDI network. Depending on their construction, these controllers allow attached devices to act as single attachment stations or dual attachment stations. Each controller has an interface to a specific workstation or system bus; for example, RISC-based TURBOchannel or other standard bus interface.

One type of FDDI controller, designed for the TURBOchannel bus, is shown in Figure 60, but several different kinds are available. Although construction and implementation vary from one controller type to another, the controller's basic function, purpose, and connection to the FDDI network remain the same.

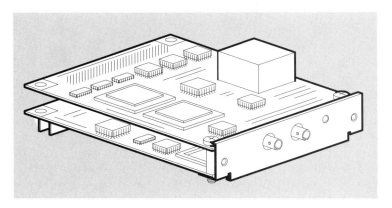

Figure 60 • An FDDI controller

The controller consists of PMD, PHY, MAC, and SMT entities. It connects to the end station's internal bus structure. An intelligent controller has onboard microprocessor-controlled logic that allows it to transfer data between the end station and the FDDI network, typically without involving the host device in which the controller resides. Connection to the FDDI network is made directly to the FDDI dual ring (DAS) or through the concentrator (SAS or DAS).

● Summary

Single attachment stations and dual attachment stations allow users to connect to the FDDI network. SAS and DAS controllers are installed in workstations, minicomputers, or other network devices to connect these devices to the FDDI network.

Single attachment stations connect to the ring through the M ports of concentrators. Dual attachment stations connect directly to the dual ring, or to the ring through a concentrator. Use of the concentrator enables bypass of failed or disconnected SAS or DAS devices for added network availability and reliability. This is especially important for mission-critical applications. The concentrator also allows dual homing of DAS devices for additional fault tolerance in the FDDI ring.

Chapter 12 • FDDI: LAN Interconnection Devices

Large networks are typically made up of numerous smaller subnetworks linked together by means of interconnecting devices such as bridges and routers. Such interconnect devices must conform to some set standards, usually IEEE 802.1d, 802.1h, and 802.1i for bridging and TCP/IP and/or OSI for routing, to ensure multivendor and multinetwork interoperability.

• Bridges

In the FDDI environment, or for that matter, any extended LAN environment, the bridge acts as a Data Link relay between networks. These LANs can be of the same type, or they can be based on two different standards. Figure 61 illustrates the connection of an FDDI LAN to a different LAN-type (IEEE 802.3/Ethernet in this instance).

Bridges are protocol-independent, specialized LAN stations. They are store-and-forward devices operating at the Data Link layer of the OSI model. Bridges can reduce total traffic on the extended LAN by filtering unnecessary traffic from the overall network.

A properly designed bridge provides a transparent link between networks. For example, users on the FDDI network can freely exchange data with users on other networks using routable and non-routable network protocols.

A major reason for choosing FDDI is that it is an open standard allowing the interchange of data among multivendor network devices. To take advantage of this open architecture, buyers should avoid components that lock them into a specific vendor implementation. Doing this may result in being tied to a closed, proprietary system with equipment choices limited to a single source. Bridges are a prime example where the wrong choice may lock users into a proprietary system.

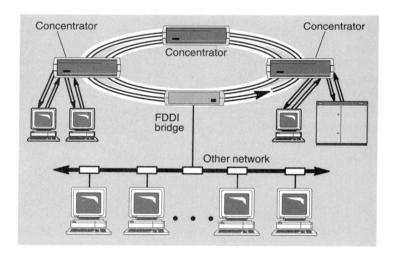

Figure 61 • Two networks connected with an FDDI bridge

• Bridge Functions

Basic FDDI-to-Ethernet bridge functions include:

• Source address tracking

• Frame forwarding and filtering

- Participation in the *spanning tree* algorithm

- Translation

- Fragmentation and segmentation

- Performance of bridge management functions

Although an FDDI bridge can have more than two ports, for simplicity the following sections deal with a two-port architecture such as that used in a two-port FDDI-to-802.3/Ethernet bridge.

Source Address Tracking

Whenever a bridge receives a frame, it records the source address of the frame into its forwarding database, also called an address lookup table. The forwarding database is simply a location in the memory of the bridge containing the data link addresses of all stations that have been seen by the bridge. It also indicates the direction from which the frame was received, or simply which side of the bridge received the frame. Bridges that can automatically build these databases are called self-learning bridges.

Because each frame contains the source address of the transmitting station, the bridge is constantly updating its forwarding database, learning the location of each station that sends a frame over the network. In an extended network, a bridge learns the locations of all stations relative to its own position in the network as frames pass through the bridge. Network management functions implemented by some vendors allow users to modify the address lookup tables.

Frame Forwarding and Filtering

As stated previously, the basic purpose of a bridge is to forward frames between its attached LANs. This allows the stations on each LAN to communicate with all other stations as if they were on one large extended LAN.

To do this forwarding effectively, bridges have store-and-forward functionality. They automatically store incoming frames and then forward only those frames destined for a station on the other side of the bridge. This is called *destination address filtering* and is done by using the address lookup tables. Frames not destined to cross the bridge are simply discarded from the bridge's storage area.

Filtering is a process where frames are prevented from crossing the bridge. There are three basic types of filtering that can be done by a bridge: destination address filtering, *source address filtering*, and *protocol filtering*. These functions perform exactly as their names imply and are discussed in the following paragraphs. All bridges perform destination address filtering, but bridges do not necessarily perform source address and protocol filtering.

Destination Address Filtering

When a message comes in from one LAN, the bridge examines the source and destination address and forwards messages that are destined for other local area networks. It filters (discards) those messages belonging on the same LAN as the transmitting station. In some bridges, network management can modify the destination address lookup tables so that the bridge will always filter, or always forward, frames destined for these addresses.

Source Address Filtering

Some bridges also perform source address filtering where messages from a designated source address are forwarded or rejected. For example, management could send the bridge a message to reject all messages sent by station B. When a message comes from station B, the bridge does not forward the message across the bridge. Alternatively the bridge could reject all messages for stations that are not listed on a specific lookup table. This is a useful device for controlling traffic flow, to isolate systems, and to provide additional security.

Protocol Filtering

Some current generation bridges now offer protocol filtering, as well as source address filtering. Here, management instructs the bridge to filter all transmissions originated under a specified protocol. In this case, the bridge forwards or filters frames based on the protocol information within the frame. This type of filtering is also useful for controlling traffic flow, to isolate systems, and to provide additional security.

Bridge Performance Considerations

To take advantage of the power of FDDI, an FDDI bridge must be capable of supporting high throughput. It should not be a bottleneck. As data passes through it, the bridge must make decisions in microseconds concerning frame destination. Key bridge performance characteristics include the filtering, forwarding, and translating rates.

Filtering Rate

The filtering rate is the speed at which the bridge processes receive frames and determines if they are to be forwarded across the bridge. A high filtering rate keeps the bridge from clogging with data frames that are not being forwarded. Efficient filtering reduces the probability of dropping a frame which should be forwarded.

Forwarding Rate

The forwarding rate is based on the number of data frames that can be transferred from one LAN to another. It should be large enough to allow a high volume of traffic between the LANs. The forwarding rate is determined by the speed of the bridge in re-transmitting the frame onto the next network after the filtering decision has been made.

Translating Rate

Translation is the ability of the bridge to convert frames of one LAN data link format to frames of a different LAN data link format. The translating rate determines the number of frames that can be forwarded between dissimilar LAN types. How quickly a bridge can accomplish this task is a key factor in determining bridge performance. The translating rate may limit the forwarding rate between dissimilar LANs.

Spanning Tree

The logical topology of an extended LAN must be loop-free. That is, there should be a single, clearly defined path among all attached stations. To prevent logical loops on the extended network, bridges form a logical configuration called a spanning tree.

Formation of a spanning tree is done based on an industry-standard spanning tree algorithm defined by IEEE 802.1d. This algorithm prevents the occurrence of logical loops in the extended network. The spanning tree algorithm has two primary functions:

• The creation of only one logical path between any two bridges

• The proper connection of all LANs into a single extended LAN with no active duplicate paths formed among connected bridges

The algorithm works by having all bridges in a given LAN exchange frames called Hello messages. The bridges use the information in these messages to select the bridges that should forward frames and those that should be idle, acting only as backups to the active paths.

Encapsulating and Translating Bridges

Some suppliers of FDDI bridges use proprietary encapsulation schemes. They did this because they assumed that:

• FDDI was to be used only as a pipeline for IEEE 802.3 or IEEE 802.5 sub-LAN traffic.

• Stations on other LANs would not need to communicate with devices on the FDDI network.

However, systems in an extended LAN have to operate together. To do this, stations on the FDDI network must be able to communicate with stations on the other networks and vice versa. *Encapsulating bridges* cannot provide this interoperability as their algorithms are proprietary to the individual bridge vendor.

In keeping with the open system philosophy of FDDI, a technique called translation is available. *Translating bridges* create frames that are standard across the interconnected LANs, thus ensuring interoperability. The translation algorithm is specified by IEEE 802.1.

Encapsulating Bridges

Using a proprietary protocol, the Ethernet-to-FDDI encapsulating bridge surrounds (encapsulates) the Ethernet frame with an FDDI *header* and *trailer*. It then forwards this frame to the FDDI network. In other words, the entire frame received from the non-FDDI network becomes the data in an FDDI frame.

The destination address is hidden in the encapsulated frame. This means that the encapsulating bridge must send the FDDI frame to another encapsulating bridge that uses the identical encapsulating technique for de-encapsulation. This usually means that only a bridge, or receiving device, supplied by the same vendor can make use of this encapsulated data (Figure 62).

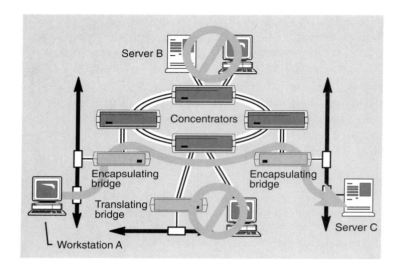

Figure 62 • Encapsulated bridging — limited access

Encapsulation severely limits interoperability in multivendor networks. For example, a workstation user on a sub-LAN can use an encapsulating bridge to get to a high-performance server on another sub-LAN. However, the encapsulating bridge does not let the user access servers or systems directly attached to the FDDI network. Figure 62 shows that Workstation A can access Server C, but cannot access Server B.

Encapsulation results in the user being forced into a closed, proprietary, single-vendor network architecture. There are no ANSI, ISO, or other accepted industry standards for encapsulation. All FDDI encapsulation schemes are proprietary and usually vendor specific.

Translating Bridges

A translating bridge modifies the fields of a forwarded frame to make it compliant with the frame format of the network to which it is being sent. The IEEE 802.1i FDDI supplement to the 802.1d bridging standard defines how bridging is accomplished between any 802 LAN and FDDI.

For example, workstations on an IEEE 802.3/Ethernet sub-LAN can use high-performance servers directly attached to FDDI networks because the IEEE 802.3/Ethernet frames are translated to FDDI frames. Figure 63 shows that Workstation A can access both Server B on another sub-LAN and Server C on the FDDI network, even if the bridges are from different vendors. In this example, an IEEE 802.3/Ethernet frame is translated into an FDDI frame to reach Server B or Server C. If the destination is on yet another LAN, the FDDI frame is translated into a format consistent with the format of the destination LAN.

Some protocols such as AppleTalk Version 2 use a frame format that is unrecognizable as it passes through IEEE 802.ld/802.li standards-based translating bridges. To handle such anomalies, the IEEE 802.lh standard for Media Access Control (MAC) Bridging of Ethernet V2.0 in 802 LANs was established to define support for non-standard protocols. IEEE 802.lh enables translating bridges to transparently handle the AppleTalk Version 2 frames.

Any translating bridge conforming to the IEEE 802.1d, 802.1h, and 802.1i standards for bridging can interoperate with any other translating bridge, yielding an open, nonproprietary solution.

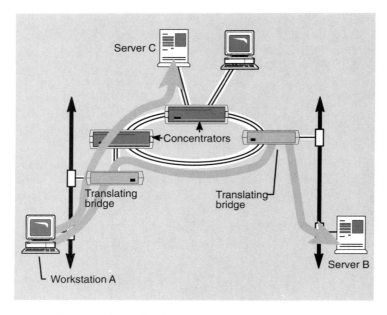

Figure 63 • Translating bridging—full access

Internet Protocol Fragmentation

FDDI permits the creation of frames up to 4500 bytes in length. Sub-LANs, such as IEEE 802.3/Ethernet, do not have the capability to handle frame sizes this large. What happens when a bridge is asked to forward a 4500 byte FDDI frame to an 802.3/Ethernet sub-LAN?

Common communication protocols, such as the Internet Protocol (IP), define a method for handling such frame size differences known as frame *fragmentation*. As shown in Figure 64, fragmentation breaks up large frames into smaller frames, each of which contains control information for re-assembly by the end-station. This ensures that frame size restrictions are not violated when frames cross FDDI-to-802.3/Ethernet boundaries. The smaller frames can then be forwarded successfully to sub-LANs.

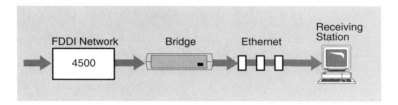

Figure 64 • Fragmentation

Some bridges have this fragmentation capability. Network planners should choose 802.3/Ethernet-to-FDDI bridges with this feature when FDDI is implemented and 802.3/Ethernet sub-LANs are present. As in address translation, however, fragmentation must be done very quickly, so as not to degrade the performance of the bridge.

Fragmentation is important for applications and protocols that use large frame sizes. Without fragmentation in an FDDI bridge, certain applications simply will not work over the bridge interconnection.

OSI Segmentation

A similar fragmentation process is being defined for OSI frames called segmentation. Since OSI segmentation continues to be defined at the time of this writing, users should select bridge products that incorporate IP fragmentation today and have the ability to easily add OSI segmentation in the future.

Bridge Management

Bridge management includes the ability to monitor conditions and implement filters on the extended network. Monitoring is done in order to adjust the logical topology for better traffic patterns or to fix things if they go wrong. For this reason, some bridges maintain counters for such things as the number of frames forwarded and discarded.

The bridge forwarding database should be able to be remotely observed and modified. This allows network management to determine the location of user stations or to manage various regions of the extended network. Also, by adjusting parameters in the spanning tree algorithm and implementing filters, a network manager can fine tune the extended LAN performance for specific topologies.

● Routers

Routers are dedicated systems on a LAN whose purpose is to offload the routing function from other network nodes in the LAN. Routers, as OSI level 3 devices, connect nodes and networks of like architecture, or link different network types that support the same network protocols. Routers provide LAN-to-LAN interconnection, either locally or across the WAN.

Routers maintain two types of information: node addresses and network status. Each router maintains an address database of other routers and of reachable end nodes. Routers periodically update these databases by exchanging status information with each other and with attached nodes. Routers also periodically exchange messages about the status of links in the network, traffic load and network topology. The information is kept in a separate database and is examined each time a frame arrives.

In a WAN, there can be multiple communication links and relay points (routers). Frames move through these links in a series of hops. Each router chooses the next link to carry the frame.

Unlike a bridge, the presence of the router in the network is known to the sending node. When a frame needs to be routed, the sending node explicitly addresses the router, asking it to route that frame (Figure 65). As the frame passes through the router, the router examines its database to identify the next router in the best path towards the destination of that frame, re-addresses the frame, and sends it to the next router.

This differs from bridging in that the bridge is transparent to the sending station. The bridge sits on the LAN watching frames and, when a frame is addressed to a station not on the LAN, it simply forwards the frame on to the next LAN. As far as the sending station knows, the destination station is on the same LAN. In this case, the format of the destination and source address in the frame stays the same (Figure 65).

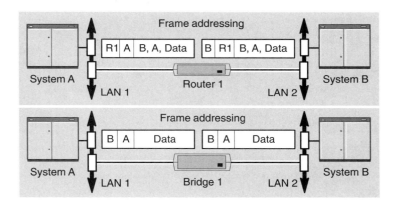

Figure 65 • Frame addressing for routing and bridging

Flow Control

Networks can operate at different data transmission rates. Routers are useful devices to control the flow of information between multiple networks. When the router is busy, it can send a "stop sending" message to the sender and other routers. This gives the router time to clear its buffers. If for some reason the router cannot deliver the frame to the next router, it holds the frame until it can be delivered.

Routers can also be used to isolate LANs from each other because they prevent LAN broadcast messages from leaving the originating LAN. Segmenting broadcast traffic is an excellent means of reducing the traffic load across multiple interconnected LANs.

• Single and Multiprotocol Routing

Each protocol typically has its own routing algorithm or rules. However, routers can be designed to operate as single or multiprotocol routers.

Single Protocol

A single protocol router routes one protocol and talks to other routers with one "routing protocol." A routing protocol is simply the language spoken by routers to exchange network status and node address information. Single protocol routers keep a single address data base.

Multiprotocol

A router that routes multiple protocols is called a multiprotocol router. A multiprotocol router must keep an address database for each protocol that it serves.

There are three ways to achieve multiprotocol routing with a single set of routers: Ships-in-the-Night, Encapsulation, and Integrated Routing.

Ships-in-the-Night

Ships-in-the-Night (SIN) multiprotocol routers use independent routing protocols for each supported protocol. For example, a SIN multiprotocol router could use DECnet for routing DECnet, OSPF or RIP (*Routing Information Protocol*) for routing TCP/IP, and ISO IS-IS for routing OSI.

OSPF (Open Shortest Path First) is the newest of these routing protocols. It is an internet standard (RFC 1247) routing protocol for TCP/IP. OSPF uses the newer *link state routing* algorithm. This routing algorithm was designed especially for the larger, more complex TCP/IP networks that are being built today.

Because each routing protocol has its own rules, implementing all the various rules in a multiprotocol router slows performance. Typically, the more protocols supported on the router, the lower the throughput (performance) of the device.

Aside from performance, the additional cost of SIN multiprotocol routing is the cost of management. Even though there is only one physical network of routers to manage, there are multiple virtual networks layered on top (one virtual network per routing protocol). Each virtual network must be managed according to the rules of the particular routing protocol. Further, each network must be tuned for optimal performance. Tuning multiple virtual networks that are riding over one set of routers and one set of links is a multivariant, complex task.

Encapsulation

In an attempt to improve performance and simplify the management of multiprotocol networks, some multiprotocol routers encapsulate messages sent between routers. Frames are encapsulated into either a proprietary protocol or into the Internet Protocol (IP).

Use of proprietary protocols to route encapsulated frames restricts the de-encapsulating router at the other end to the same vendor to make the communication work. And even if the standard Internet Protocol is used as the encapsulating protocol, if the encapsulation scheme used by the router vendor is proprietary, then the de-encapsulating router still needs to be from the same vendor. This is identical to the bridge encapsulation problem.

Integrated Routing

In light of the limitations resulting from Ships-in-the-Night and Encapsulation multiprotocol routing, some vendors are implementing integrated routing protocols. As the name implies, an integrated routing protocol serves multiple protocols. Standard integrated routing protocols allow for one network—physical and virtual—to be built using routers from multiple vendors. The advantages gained are better performance, simplified management, and choice of routing vendor throughout the network.

Integrated Intermediate System-to-Intermediate System (Integrated IS-IS) has emerged as a standard routing protocol. The Integrated IS-IS protocol is specified in two documents from two standards-setting groups:

- OSI Intra-Domain IS-IS standard (ISO 10589)

- Internet Engineering Task Force (IETF) Request for Comment (RFC) 1195

Integrated IS-IS is an extension of the ISO standard IS-IS routing protocol. It allows for three types of routing:

- Pure IP

- Pure OSI

- Dual (IP and OSI)

Integrated IS-IS and OSPF are very similar routing protocols. They both use the link state routing algorithm—ideal for large, complex networks. The major difference between these two routing protocols is that Integrated IS-IS is "integrated," serving more than one protocol, while OSPF serves only TCP/IP.

• Summary

SAS and DAS devices called bridges and routers provide the means to connect FDDI LANs with other LANs.

Bridges act as links between local area networks in an extended LAN environment. Important bridge features are:

- Translation according to the IEEE 802.lh and 802.li standards

- Conformance to the IEEE 802.ld spanning tree algorithm

- Source address, protocol, and destination address filtering

- Internet Protocol fragmentation

Routers are dedicated devices used to route messages between systems. Key points to remember about routers include:

- Routers can provide flow control on a network.

- Routing permits the use of alternate paths for flow control and load balancing.

- Routers can be either single protocol or multiprotocol.

- Multiprotocol routers that use standard integrated routing protocols provide optimal performance, manageability, and allow for multivendor, multiprotocol networks.

Finally, to provide investment protection and for future growth, choose only nonproprietary LAN interconnect devices when planning an FDDI network.

Chapter 13 • Network Management: A Global View

A network management system provides a framework for the management of heterogeneous, multivendor systems. These systems can be linked to a number of network environments. The ability to manage devices over an extended network provides users with tremendous flexibility in terms of network design and cost savings.

An effective network management system lets network personnel meet specific organizational goals and technical needs. Network management allows network personnel to effectively design, implement, and maintain networks.

Without sophisticated and flexible management software, even the most powerful network can become an unwieldy, hard-to-use system.

• Management Tools

Network management tools provide an integrated, extendable approach to management. These tools offer the following benefits:

- Flexibility

- Integration

- Growth potential

Another benefit is protection of the network investment. Because existing components, as well as any new additions, are supported, there is no need to discard existing equipment when expanding network facilities.

• Role of FDDI Station Management

The frame-based services section of Station Management (SMT) defines a protocol that addresses the management of specific portions of the FDDI standards (Figure 66).

As defined in the FDDI standards, SMT manages the Physical Layer Medium Dependent, Physical Layer Protocol, and Media Access Control portions of FDDI. It is currently being modified and finalized by ANSI.

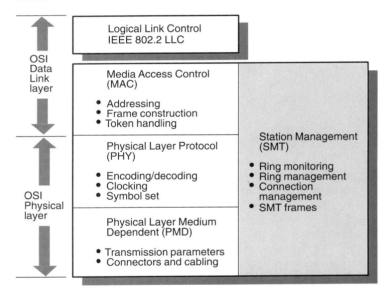

Figure 66 • Role of Station Management

FDDI SMT frames are limited to use on a single FDDI ring. They cannot be used across a wide area network or across multiple FDDI rings. They also cannot be used to manage functions outside of FDDI, for example, IEEE 802.3 and IEEE 802.5 networks.

• Simple Network Management Protocol

Simple Network Management Protocol (SNMP) is an application layer, standards-based protocol for network management. Developed by the *Internet Engineering Task Force* (IETF), SNMP provides access to FDDI counters and control functions for network management applications in TCP/IP environments.

Applications using SNMP communicate over a wide area network or across multiple rings or LANs. SNMP management stations can manage other functions (outside of FDDI) within a network, such as IEEE 802.3/Ethernet bridges or routers, wide area routers, or systems.

• Common Management Information Protocol

Common Management Information Protocol (CMIP) is an application layer, OSI-based protocol for system and network management. CMIP enables open systems communication in an OSI environment. Like SNMP, CMIP can be used to manage a broad range of system and network objects. This protocol is growing in popularity across the telecommunications industry where OSI is being embraced.

• Management Functions

Management functions are used by network- and system-level personnel to monitor, control, and maintain the network. As set forth in the ISO/OSI management framework, these functions consist of the following:

• Configuration management

• Fault management

• Performance management

• Accounting management

• Security management

Users should be able to customize management functions to support their requirements. The functions should interact so that the output of one function can be input to another. This provides support of the network systems throughout their existence, from planning and implementation to operation and change.

Figure 67 shows an example of a network management system.

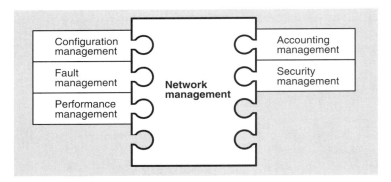

Figure 67 • Network management system example

Configuration Management

Configuration management allows users to set or change operating parameters of the local or extended network. This includes the ability to turn the parameters on or off or alter their operational status. It also includes the ability to collect and distribute current status information of attached devices.

As part of configuration management, ring mapping allows users to identify all devices on the local or extended network. The entire network configuration can be mapped providing network managers valuable network status information.

Fault Management

Fault management provides a means to detect, diagnose, and correct network faults and error conditions. It includes:

• Receipt of unsolicited error messages from network devices

• Periodic polling for error messages

• Setting error thresholds for individual devices

Through proper setting and monitoring of operational parameters, network managers can prevent certain fault conditions. Examples of this include error alarms and threshold limits.

Performance Management

Performance management lets the network manager monitor and evaluate network performance. With this facility, managers check the performance of the local and extended networks. Data is gathered from device counters and error reports. Information is then processed and analyzed for network planning and tuning.

Accounting Management

Accounting management allows managers to effectively monitor and evaluate network resources and their use. This application function identifies usage costs associated with the network. It also provides the necessary tools for identifying and charging users for network time.

Security Management

The ability to create a secure environment is increasing in importance for two reasons: networks are becoming larger and more complex; and, companies are placing highly sensitive data on the network. Security management defines facilities required to authenticate data and users, control access to resources, and protect confidential information on both the local and extended networks.

● Summary

A network management system provides a framework for the management of heterogeneous, multivendor systems.

SMT is an FDDI-specific management protocol that can be used to manage a single FDDI LAN. SNMP is a network management protocol used to manage FDDI, 802.3, and 802.5 LANs as well as WANs.

Large, complex networks should be managed by industry-standard protocols, like SNMP or CMIP. Such protocols allow management of many devices among diverse local and wide area network types from a centralized network management system.

Management functions are used by network- and system-level personnel to monitor, control, and maintain the network. A comprehensive network management system provides for configuration, fault, performance, accounting, and security management.

The IEEE 802.3, IEEE 802.5, and FDDI LAN standards are the most commonly used LAN standards. The IEEE 802.3 standard defines a logical bus topology using the *Carrier Sense Multiple Access with Collision Detection* (CSMA/CD) access method. The IEEE 802.5 standard defines a token passing ring architecture, which can operate at either 4 or 16 Mbps. The FDDI standard defines a 100 Mbps token passing ring, based on a timed token protocol. Each of these standards is used with the IEEE 802.2 LLC protocol, and the IEEE 802.1 higher layer protocols. Figure 68 shows the relationship of these LAN standards to each other and the ISO/OSI model.

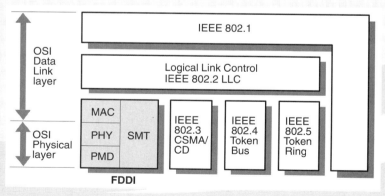

Figure 68 • Relationship of FDDI and other LAN standards

There are many differences among the FDDI, IEEE 802.3, and IEEE 802.5 standards. These differences range from the type of media to:

• How fast a message can be sent

• How far apart stations can be on the network

• How the station gains the right to send a message

• How the station encodes a message for transmission over the media

• How the station sends a message

• How large a single message can be

The FDDI, IEEE 802.3, and IEEE 802.5 standards also define different logical and physical topologies.

• Bandwidth

Bandwidth is a measure of the amount of traffic that can be transmitted on the network at one time. In purely digital communications, bandwidth describes the amount of data that can be transmitted over the line in bits per second (i.e., the data rate). Table 3 compares the bandwidth specified by the FDDI, IEEE 802.3, and IEEE 802.5 standards.

Table 3 • Comparison of bandwidth

	FDDI	**IEEE 802.3**	**IEEE 802.5**
Bandwidth	100 Mb/s	10 Mb/s	4 or 16 Mb/s

• Number of Stations and Distances

Local area network standards specify the maximum number of stations permitted on the network. They also specify the distance between stations and the maximum total extent of the network.

Table 4 compares the maximum number of stations, maximum distance between stations, and maximum network extent for the FDDI, IEEE 802.3, and IEEE 802.5 standards.

Table 4 • Comparison of maximum number of stations and distances

	FDDI	**IEEE 802.3**	**IEEE 802.5**
Number of stations	500	1024	250
Maximum distance between stations	2 km (1.2 mi) MMF or > 20 km (>12.4 mi) SMF	2.8 km (1.7 mi)	300 m (984 ft) station to wiring closet (4 Mb/s ring); however, 100 m (328 ft) is recommended for both 4 and 16 Mb/s
Maximum network extent	100 km (62 mi)	2.8 km (1.7 mi)	Varies with configuration

MMF=Multimode fiber
SMF=Single-mode fiber

● **Network Topology**

Network topologies are described in two ways: logical topologies and physical topologies. Logical topologies describe the view of the network as seen by the station's access method (i.e., its rules of operation). Physical topologies define the layout of the wiring. The IEEE 802.3, IEEE 802.5, and FDDI standards define different logical topologies, but all of them can be mapped onto the EIA/TIA 568 physical topology rules.

IEEE 802.3 defines a logical bus. All stations are connected to the bus, but that bus can be implemented as a hierarchy of repeaters that connect stations via different media types.

IEEE 802.5 defines *logical ring* topologies in which the token circulates from station to station. The rings may be implemented as a hierarchy of *Multistation Access Units*, connecting stations with different media types.

Finally, FDDI is also a logical ring topology, in which concentrators form a dual ring of trees physical topology, connecting stations to the ring.

Table 5 compares the topologies specified by the FDDI, IEEE 802.3, and IEEE 802.5 standards.

Table 5 ● Comparison of topologies

	FDDI	**IEEE 802.3**	**IEEE 802.5**
Logical topology	Dual ring, Dual ring of trees	Bus	Single ring
Physical topology	Ring, Star, Hierarchical star	Star, Bus, Hierarchical star	Ring, Star Hierarchical star

• Supported Media

The connection between stations is comprised of some form of physical media, such as twisted pair cable or optical fiber. All three network technologies are capable of supporting many media types.

The current media supported by the standards are listed in Table 6. While each of the standards support a variety of media types, the specific transmission characteristics of each of the media differ between each standard. Before designing your network, it is crucial to ensure that the cable you have will be capable of supporting the desired network technology. Trained network installers can help you to make this determination.

Table 6 • Comparison of media

	FDDI	**IEEE 802.3**	**IEEE 802.5**
Media	Optical fiber	Optical fiber, Twisted-pair, Coaxial cable	Twisted-pair, Optical fiber

While some vendors offer other media types (coaxial, shielded and unshielded twisted-pair) for FDDI solutions, these were not included in the table since they are not yet defined by the FDDI standards committee.

• Media Access Method

Which stations gain access to the media is determined by the access method. Access methods mediate between stations that are competing for use of the medium. The FDDI, IEEE 802.3, and IEEE 802.5 standards differ in the way in which stations gain access to the network media.

IEEE 802.3 CSMA/CD

The IEEE 802.3 standard access method is referred to as the Carrier Sense Multiple Access with Collision Detection (CSMA/CD) method. The name describes the method very well. Carrier Sense — A station listens to the channel prior to transmitting to detect the presence of other transmissions, or carriers. If it determines that no other transmissions are present, it begins sending its frame. Multiple Access — Up to 1024 stations share the logical bus, which means that there is access by multiple stations. Collision Detection — *Propagation delays* between stations mean that two stations might begin a transmission, believing that the channel was clear. When these two signals encounter each other on the cable, a collision is said to have occurred. Stations detect the collision and wait a random amount of time before retransmitting their data. The random backoff, as it is called, means that the stations will retransmit at different times, avoiding a second collision. Figure 69 shows how CSMA/CD works.

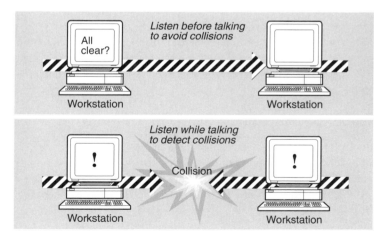

Figure 69 ● Carrier sense multiple access with collision detection

IEEE 802.5 Token Ring

The IEEE 802.5 standard access method is based on token ring technology. Ring initialization and token generation are done by a master system. A token grants its holder the right to transmit for a period of time defined by the token holding rules. A token circulates around the ring in-between transmissions (see Figure 70). When a stations wishes to transmit, it:

- Captures the token

- Changes a bit within the token to mark the token busy, thus converting the token to a start-of-frame sequence

- Transmits one frame

Other stations repeat the bits of the frame, with each station in turn passing the bits to its downstream neighbor. One or more of the stations may choose to receive the frame by making a copy of it as it passes through the station on its way around the ring. When the transmitting station sees its own frame return, it removes the frame from the ring, and then issues a new token after the last bit of the transmitted frame has been removed from the network.

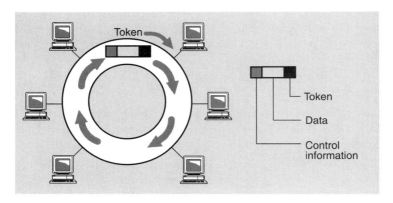

Figure 70 • IEEE 802.5 token passing method

Note that the above description refers to the operation of the 4 Mb/s token ring. In the IEEE 802.5 standard 4 Mb/s ring, there can be one token and data frames from only one station on the ring. The station releases the token after it strips all the frames from the ring. The token passing technique in IEEE 802.5 4 Mb/s is not as efficient in its use of bandwidth as FDDI.

An enhancement of the 4 Mb/s method was adopted for the 16 Mb/s token ring. In this case, the station can issue the new token as soon as it finishes transmitting its frame. This method, known as "early token release," enables better utilization of the ring by allowing one token and one frame each from multiple systems and stations on the ring at a time. It accomplishes this by allowing the next station to transmit without incurring the delay needed for the original transmitter to finish removing its frame from the ring.

FDDI

FDDI is also a token passing ring technology, but its rules are tailored to make sure that the token is available to each station within an agreed upon time limit. This time limit is negotiated by the stations each time that a new station joins the ring. In FDDI, a station transmits by first capturing the token. It then transmits as many frames as is allowed by the token rules. In most cases this means that many frames are transmitted. After the frames are transmitted, the station immediately reissues a token. One or more stations can copy the frame as it passes through their station. The transmitted frames are repeated from station to station on the ring, until they return to the sender, which removes them from the ring.

Only one token can be present on the ring at a time, but multiple frames from multiple systems or stations can be on the ring. The timed-token passing technique is an efficient use of bandwidth. (Refer to Chapter 7 for more information.)

Table 7 compares the media access methods for the FDDI, IEEE 802.3, and IEEE 802.5 standards.

Table 7 • Comparison of media access methods

	FDDI	**IEEE 802.3**	**IEEE 802.5**
Access Method	Timed-token passing	CSMA/CD	Token passing
Token acquisition	Captures the token	Not applicable (CSMA/CD)	By setting a status bit, converts token into a frame
Token release	After transmit	Not applicable (CSMA/CD)	After stripping (4) or after transmit (16)
Frames on LAN	Multiple	Single	1 (4 Mb/s rings) or multiple (16 Mb/s rings)
Frames transmitted per access	Multiple	Single	Single

• Frame Size

Once a station obtains a turn to transmit, the actual amount of data transmitted is controlled by the size of the data unit and the speed at which it can be transmitted.

Data is transmitted in frames over the medium. As shown in Table 8, the maximum frame size differs among FDDI, IEEE 802.3, and IEEE 802.5.

Table 8 • Comparison of frame size

	FDDI	**IEEE 802.3**	**IEEE 802.5.**
Maximum frame size	4,500 bytes	1,518 bytes	4,500 bytes (4) 17,800 bytes (16)

• Summary

FDDI includes a wealth of features that makes it well-suited for growing businesses. The differences among the FDDI, IEEE 802.3, and IEEE 802.5 LAN standards are important to network managers when they plan, implement, and maintain networks. These differences range from the type of media to how large a single frame can be, to how far apart stations can be on the network.

Table 9 summarizes the differences and similarities among the FDDI, IEEE 802.3, and IEEE 802.5 standards.

Table 9 • Summary, comparison among standards

	FDDI	**IEEE 802.3**	**IEEE 802.5**
Bandwidth	100 Mb/s	10 Mb/s	4 or 16 Mb/s
Number stations	500	1024	250
Maximum distance between stations	2 km (1.2 mi) MMF or > 20 km (> 12.4 mi) SMF	2.8 km (1.7 mi)	300 m (984 ft) station to wiring closet (4 Mb/s ring); however, 100 m (328 ft) is recommended for both 4 and 16 Mb/s
Maximum network extent	100 km (62 mi)	2.8 km (1.7 mi)	Varies with configuration
Logical topology	Dual ring, Dual ring of trees	Bus	Single ring
Physical topology	Ring, Star, Hierarchical star	Star, Bus, Hierarchical star	Ring, Star Hierarchical star
Media	Optical fiber	Optical fiber, Twisted-pair, Coaxial cable	Twisted-pair, Optical fiber

Table 9 • Summary, comparison among standards (cont.)

Access method	Timed-token passing	CSMA/CD	Token passing
Token acquisition	Captures the token	Not applicable (CSMA/CD)	By setting a status bit, converts token into a frame
Token release	After transmit	Not applicable (CSMA/CD)	After stripping (4) or after transmit (16)
Frames on LAN	Multiple	Single	1 (4 Mb/s rings) or multiple (16 Mb/s rings)
Frames transmitted per access	Multiple	Single	Single
Maximum frame size	4,500 bytes	1,518 bytes	4,500 bytes (4) or 17,800 bytes (16)

MMF=Multimode fiber
SMF=Single-mode fiber

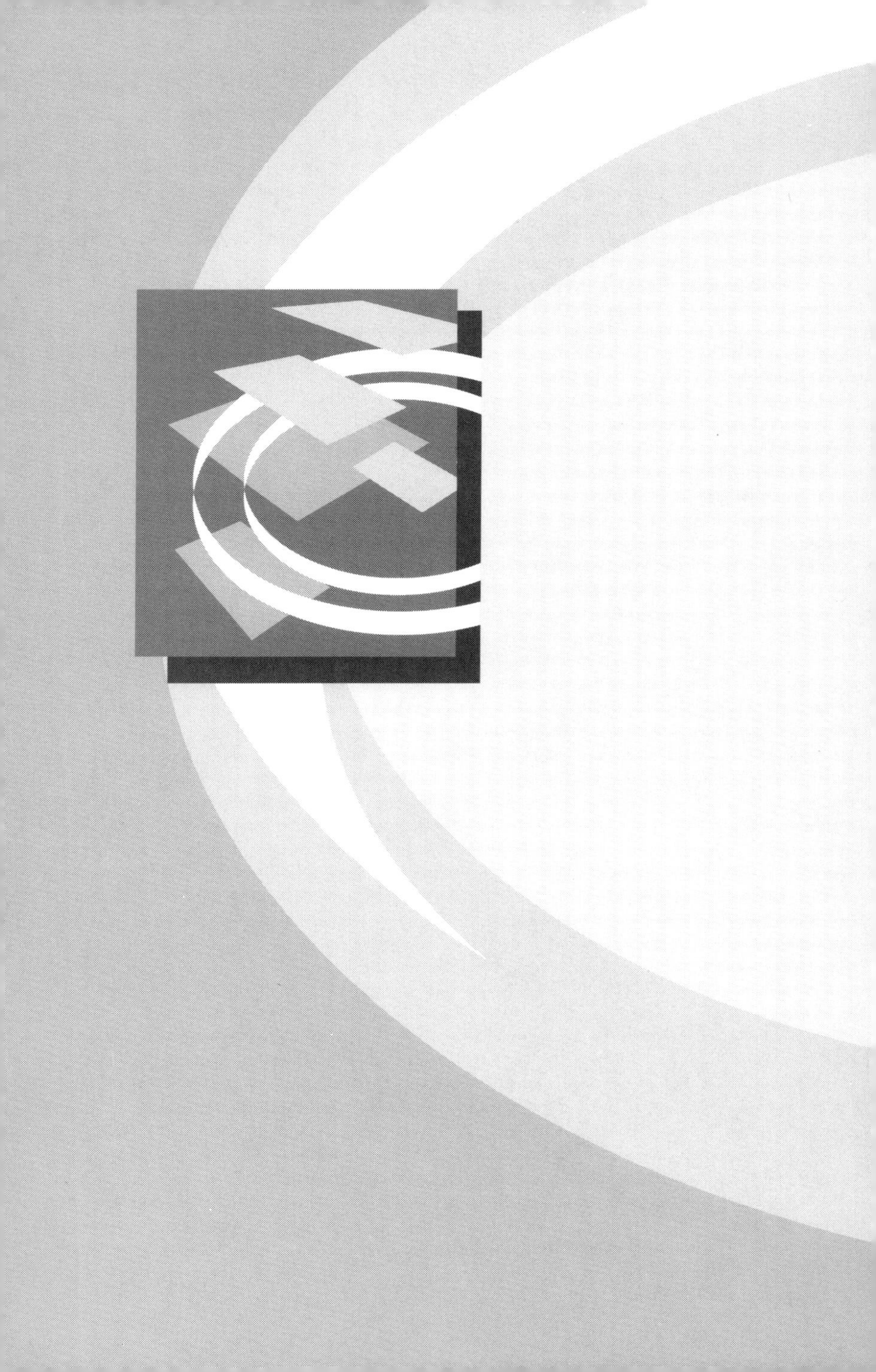

Chapter 15 • Implementing FDDI: Considerations

Today's facility-wide networks contain products and technologies that are produced by many different vendors. The majority of networks are based on the IEEE 802.3 standard. However, the IEEE 802.5 token ring standard is gaining in popularity.

The IEEE 802.3 standard has attained a multivendor status. A large part of its success is based on the fact that it:

- Is available from many vendors

- Offers simple-to-install and easy-to-use multivendor networking solutions

Until FDDI reaches a multivendor status similar to 802.3/Ethernet, users should select vendors that ensure compliance to the standard. This provides the best chance of ensuring multivendor interoperability.

• The Decision for FDDI

Determining if and when to implement an FDDI network depends on the following factors:

- Type of LAN applications used by the organization

- Current extent of LAN use

- Predictions on the nature of future LAN applications

- Predictions on future volume of LAN traffic

• Investment Protection

Organizations have invested significant amounts of money in the IEEE 802.3 and IEEE 802.5 technologies. Any move to FDDI networks must be based on considerations that protect these investments.

Because FDDI coexists with and is complementary to other LAN standards, the investment in these technologies is protected. The move to FDDI is made gradually as the organization needs the benefits of high-speed networking (Figure 71).

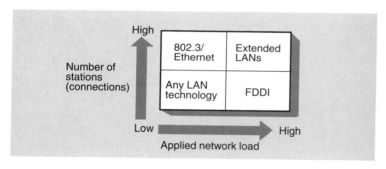

Figure 71 • Investment protection in LAN technologies

• Before Implementing FDDI

Questions relating to current LAN use can be answered accurately only by a thorough analysis of current levels of traffic. Prediction of future traffic volumes must be based on trend analysis of current traffic patterns.

Collection and interpretation of information relating to these questions falls to network management. Adopting a comprehensive approach to network management is the first step toward making an intelligent and informed decision about FDDI implementation.

Network Performance Monitoring

Understanding the traffic flow and performance of the current network is critical to a sound implementation of FDDI. Such information needs to be available continuously and in an easily readable form, so that the network planner can make informed decisions.

- If performance levels are not acceptable due to inefficient topologies, the network manager reconfigures the network.

- If poor performance is a result of inadequate bandwidth, higher bandwidth technology is required.

At this point, the network manager makes some decisions relating to investment in high-performance technologies.

High-traffic and high-security segments provide the impetus and justification for implementing FDDI. The important first step is identifying them.

Trend Analysis

Trend analysis is a critical network management function. It lets managers make intelligent predictions about the future based on analysis of current data. It is imperative for a network manager to have some idea of what to expect.

The network manager must be able to predict network activity in the immediate future, as well as three to five years from the present time. Trend analysis is possible using polled data about station and circuit activity collected over a long period.

Some vendor's network management tools perform protracted polling of stations and circuits to determine activity levels and patterns of traffic.

● FDDI Implementation

There are certain steps to follow after the need for high bandwidth and FDDI is established.

● Determine the configuration and extent of the existing cabling system.

Fiber is already in use today within IEEE 802.3 and IEEE 802.5 networks. Bridge devices in extended LANs are often linked to fiber-optic cable. This is particularly true when the distance between LANs exceeds the limit of coaxial cable.

● Develop a cable strategy if none exists.

● Pull the cable within a building, during building construction or network installation.

● If fiber is to be used in the work area, bring it to the work area on an as-needed basis by running fiber-optic cable from the wiring closets to the wall outlets in user offices.

These steps assume the use of the hierarchical EIA/TIA 568 wiring standard.

Cabling Strategy

Designing the physical cable plant requires careful planning. It should include application and connection requirements at least ten years into the future. If a well thought-out cabling strategy is implemented, the network can change and grow as the organization does.

Developing the Cable Plant

The criteria for developing and implementing a structured cable plant are based on the following:

- Ability to grow and change with the user's networking environment

- Universal multivendor capability

- Good capital investment

- Easy maintenance and service

- Flexibility, so it can be easily reconfigured in a nondisruptive manner

The network analysis process determines the network's logical configuration for the site and individual subsystems. The site's size, anticipated growth, and existing or planned buildings affect the communication needs for the site. The logical network design takes into consideration the:

- Different types of data communication services

- Network performance requirements

- Active network hardware

Certification is a post-installation procedure. Certification establishes that the installation is within the guidelines of the cable plant requirements. Fiber-optic cable plant certification is performed in two steps: optical power-loss measurements, and then splice and connector qualification.

● The Challenge for the Network Planner

Network planners face a wide range of choices when they choose FDDI components to build an open backbone system. A prime consideration is the interconnection of multivendor equipment. When planning for the backbone system, network planners need to:

● Choose vendors that provide a platform for a nonproprietary open solution

● Understand the:
  – Role and technology of bridges and routers that tie FDDI networks to sub-LANs
  – Difference between SAS and DAS devices and the advantages of concentrators
  – Advantages of the dual ring of trees topology and dual homing, a fault-tolerant technique
  – FDDI management options
  – Media alternatives
  – Differences between FDDI and *FDDI-II*

Proprietary Solutions

A proprietary solution in the backbone system can be costly because it:

● Leads to reliance on a single vendor for networking solutions

● Prevents the organization from responding to evolving networking needs and new technologies

Upgrades in a proprietary system are done with unit swap-outs or software changes. The move to an open system usually requires replacement of major components and disrupts service while the changes take place.

Nonproprietary Systems

Nonproprietary solutions include components from a single vendor or from many vendors. Nonproprietary components interoperate with each other, provided they comply with the LAN standards.

Upgrades should be done through software changes, thus providing flexibility and investment protection.

Single-vendor networking solutions provide quality service and support when they are nonproprietary. With an open system, the organization can select an alternative or second-source vendor to respond to evolving technology.

Choosing Bridges or Routers for FDDI

The features of the current generation of routers and bridges frequently overlap. Many products incorporate features of both product types. There are still distinctly different uses for each type in LAN-to-LAN connection.

- Use bridges for the LAN-to-LAN interconnection when the requirements are for low delay, high throughput, and when non-routable protocols are used.

- Use routers for the LAN-to-LAN interconnection when a high degree of isolation or flow control is required.

Figure 72 shows a centrally managed, high-performance server on the FDDI LAN. In this application, several IEEE 802.3-based CAD/CAM workgroups use the server. A high-performance 802.3/Ethernet-to-FDDI bridge provides unconstrained access to the server.

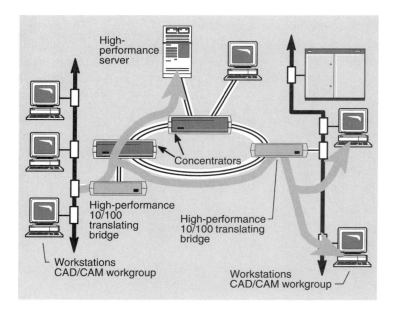

Figure 72 • Bridging to FDDI backbone

FDDI bridges are typically hybrid bridges that implement many of the same features available in multiprotocol LAN-to-LAN routers such as protocol filtering, source address filtering, packet fragmentation, and translation.

Bridges that support the IEEE 802.1d, 802.lh, and 802.1i transparent bridging standards interoperate with other bridges that also comply with these standards. Routers that use standard routing protocols, such as OSPF and Integrated IS-IS, interoperate across LANs with other routers using standard routing protocols. Standards must be used to avoid becoming vendor-dependent for new networking products.

Most LAN environments today comprise both bridges and routers. Since there are a few extensively used non-routable protocols (e.g., LAT), router-only solutions are not viable. Since many users want a high degree of isolation between specific sections of their LAN, bridge-only solutions are not viable.The correct solution for most LANs is a combination of bridges and routers.

Advantages of Using the Concentrator

The FDDI concentrator moves the responsibility of network configuration from the user into the equipment room. It lets any number of users unplug or turn off their stations. It also eliminates the possibility of a local mistake changing the global LAN topology. The user has one cable. If the cable is incorrectly plugged in, it affects only that user.

Management of the campus network is much easier when concentrators are installed. When a station or building disconnects from the LAN, the FDDI concentrator reconfigures to accommodate the change in topology. Any number of disconnected stations is allowed.The concentrator eliminates the need for many manual changes to the network topology.

After the FDDI concentrator is installed, there is never a need to coordinate activity in different buildings. Stations can disconnect at any time. A new station can be added at any time. The local concentrator reconfigures to exclude the disconnected station or include the new station.

Concentrators simplify network management. Simplified network management and topological flexibility are major reasons for using the FDDI concentrator instead of DAS devices.

Dual-ring topologies belong in the backbone where they are needed most. Dual ring of trees topologies allow flexibility in both backbone and workgroup environments. Dual attachment concentrators support dual ring, tree, and dual ring of trees topologies.

Advantages of the Dual Ring of Trees Solution

The dual ring implemented at the root of the tree delivers high availability by providing a redundant transmission path to attached concentrators, bridges, and routers. The single-ring cabling between concentrators and SAS/DAS devices or other concentrators on the tree branches provides the required scalability and maintainability of a network utility. These factors provide the robustness not found in the other topologies.

Availability

To optimize network availability, the recommended solution is to only attach network backbone devices such as concentrators, bridges, and routers directly to the dual ring. All other SAS or DAS devices should connect to the FDDI network through concentrators. The use of a concentrator connection provides more manageable, flexible solutions that isolate both the backbone and workgroup resources from service disruption.

FDDI backbone devices take advantage of the redundant feature of the FDDI dual ring to maintain network availability. And, because they are under the control of the network manager and not the end-user, the possibility of multiple segmented rings is minimized.

The SAS end-user and concentrator combination provides increased FDDI network availability by isolating end-user actions from the LAN. Since the network is unaffected by single or multiple-point failures, it is always available to attached stations. And, the dual ring of trees allows any number of stations to be removed from the ring without denying ring availability to the remaining attached stations.

Scalability

Increasing or decreasing network size is a simple matter of adding or removing concentrators. In a properly cabled site, the scale of the network is determined by the needs of the user, not the requirements of the ring topology.

The inherent flexibility of the concentrator allows network growth to be determined by the user. The dual ring of trees permits additions, moves, and changes without disruption to the network (Figure 73). This flexibility in wiring is in accordance with the wiring scheme specified in the EIA/TIA 568 standard.

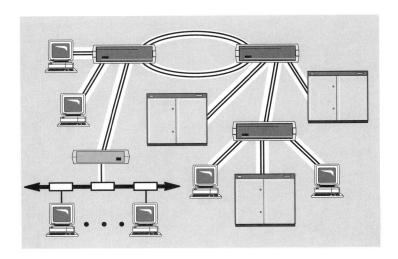

Figure 73 • A network that can grow

Maintainability

When concentrators are used, control of the ring topology is removed from the individual stations and placed in the concentrator, thus simplifying the network manager's job. Network managers use the FDDI concentrator to alter the network topology by selectively removing or inserting attached stations. Additional concentrators are easily added to the network as the organization grows.

Intelligent concentrators and distributed networking tools let the user monitor and maintain the network. Installation in dedicated equipment rooms allows careful control and maintenance of the concentrators.

Dual Homing

As you look at the tree and dual ring of trees topologies, you can see that it is possible for a concentrator to fail or for a cable to break between two concentrators or two DAS devices in the dual ring. In either event, all devices in the tree below the fiber break or failing device would no longer have access to the FDDI dual-ring network.

To prevent these potential occurrences from disrupting communications in the tree or dual ring of trees topologies, FDDI employs a fault-tolerant technique called dual homing, which is described in Chapter 9. By implementing dual homing in a tree of concentrators, devices on the tree side of a failing component can still access the FDDI ring through a backup connection to the ring.

Dual homing is an important consideration in FDDI LANs where network uptime must be maximized. The redundant device connections provided by dual homing reduce the possibility for what might be a single point of failure in tree topologies.

Selecting Network Management for FDDI

SMT's capabilities were discussed in Chapter 6, but it is important to understand SMT's limitations:

- SMT frame services are limited to use on a single FDDI LAN and, therefore, cannot be used across multiple FDDI LANs, mixed extended LANs (IEEE and FDDI), or wide area networks (WANs).

- SMT can only manage the FDDI components and functions within a station.

On the other hand, higher level protocols, such as the Simple Network Management Protocol (SNMP) or Common Management Information Protocol (CMIP), can not only provide access to FDDI counters and control functions, but these protocols can also be used to manage many other aspects of the extended LAN. Since most networks are comprised of more than a single FDDI LAN, SNMP and other higher layer management protocols will control FDDI and provide a higher degree of network manageability than is currently possible with SMT.

Alternative Media for FDDI

For some users, the move to FDDI will be determined by the installed media type, cost of installing new media, and cost of FDDI equipment (controllers, concentrators, and so forth). FDDI over copper cable is a technology that promises to lower the cost of (and thus promote) FDDI implementations. As we discussed in Chapter 3, a standard for STP and UTP is under development by the ANSI X3T9.5 Committee. Several technical issues remain to be resolved by this committee including selection of an encoding scheme, achievable distances, and determining UTP cable categories that can be supported.

An interim, interoperable STP specification co-developed by Advanced Micro Devices, Chipcom Corporation, Digital Equipment Corporation, Motorola, Inc., and SynOptics Communications, Inc. has enabled vendors to develop STP-based FDDI products in advance of a standard. This specification, known as the "Green Book," is publicly available from these vendors. Products built to the specification allow users to take advantage of FDDI's 100 Mb/s capability using their installed STP wiring today.

UTP comprises a much larger percentage of installed wiring than STP. It is the least expensive media, has the lowest installation cost, and is the simplest to install. For these reasons, coupled with the large installed base, the ability of vendors to provide users with a low-cost, reliable standards-based FDDI-over-UTP solution will be instrumental in determining the speed with which FDDI to the desktop is implemented.

FDDI vs. FDDI-II

FDDI-II is under consideration by the ANSI X3T9.5 Committee as a superset of FDDI. FDDI-II does not run any faster than FDDI—both technologies define a 100 Mb/s data transmission rate. The real difference is the intent of FDDI-II to offer *isochronous transmission* services to users on the network—services which FDDI-II proponents claim are required to support multimedia applications such as voice and video. The current evidence, however, does not support this claim.

Broadcast quality video requires a data rate which exceeds the capacity of FDDI-II or FDDI. But when the video signal is compressed, as it will be with pending standards, video traffic will become more bursty in nature than it is now, eliminating the effectiveness of isochronous services. Isochronous services, in fact, may prove to be unsuited to compressed network video activity.

Products supporting simultaneous video, voice, and data across an FDDI backbone using compression and noncompression techniques are available today. This proves that FDDI, as it is implemented today, has enough bandwidth to support compressed full-motion video, audio, and other multimedia applications across a data network. These multimedia applications (audio-video mail, voice annotation on image, and so forth) will continue to become common between networked systems using today's FDDI technology.

• Summary

The decision to implement FDDI depends on current use and predicted future use, network size, and traffic flow on the network. When implementing FDDI, careful consideration should also be given to the cable plant. A structured cable plant provides a sound foundation for flexible network topologies.

When choosing components to implement an FDDI network, network planners need to avoid proprietary solutions. They also need to understand the differences between bridges and routers, SAS and DAS devices, and the role of concentrators and SMT.

Bridges and routers both have their place in a network. Use bridges when the requirement is for low delay and nonroutable protocols. Use routers when a high degree of isolation or control is required.

DAS workstation connections may be appropriate for small workgroups, but SAS and concentrator connections provide manageability, reliability, and the ability to expand the network as the demand increases.

The dual ring of trees topology is the recommended topology because it protects the backbone from multiple failures, grows as the demand increases, and is easily maintained.

Dual homing provides fault-tolerant capabilities for the FDDI network. Through the use of redundant connections, dual homing improves the network's reliability while taking advantage of the benefits of tree and dual ring of trees topologies.

Network management is an enterprise-wide consideration. Today's business environment mandates the ability to manage the entire network. Protocols such as SNMP and CMIP allow multivendor, multistandard management without locking users into proprietary schemes.

FDDI signalling over STP and UTP copper media is under consideration by the ANSI Committee as a future standard. Given the proliferation of copper wiring in cable plants, support for this media type promises to accelerate the acceptance of FDDI to the desktop. Many technical issues, however, need to be resolved by ANSI, particularly for UTP, before a standard is available.

FDDI-II is an evolving standard that is under development by the ANSI X3T9.5 Committee and is intended to support audio, voice, video, and data applications. These applications, however, are supported by FDDI today, thus raising the question as to the benefit of a second 100 Mb/s standard.

Glossary

4B/5B: The FDDI coding scheme which maps 4 bits of hexadecimal data to a 5-bit sequence of code bits, called a code group.

American National Standards Institute: An organization that coordinates and publishes standards for use in the United States.

ANSI: *See* American National Standards Institute

asynchronous transmission: A service class provided by FDDI in which unreserved bandwidth is made available to the token holder. Data transmission is initiated by the token holder if the token holding timer has not expired.

attenuation: The amount of optical power (or light) that is lost as the light travels from the transmitter through the medium to the receiver. The difference between transmitted and received power, expressed in decibels (dB).

backbone: A network configuration that connects various LANs together into an integrated network, as for example, in a campus environment.

backend: A network configuration that connects large hosts (mainframe-type systems) to each other or to peripherals.

bandwidth: In digital communications, describes the amount of data that can be transmitted over a channel in bits-per-second.

beacon: A specialized frame used by Media Access Control to announce to other stations that the ring is broken.

bridge: An intelligent, protocol-independent, store-and-forward device that operates as a Data Link layer relay. Used to connect similar or dissimilar LANs. LANs connected by bridges are referred to as an extended LAN.

broadcast storm: A condition in which network congestion occurs because large numbers of frames are transmitted by many stations in response to a transmission by one station.

building backbone subsystem: Provides the link between the building and campus backbone. This subsystem consists of an intermediate crossconnect located in an equipment room and the cables that connect it to the telecommunications crossconnect.

bypass: The function that allows a station to be optically or electronically isolated from the network while maintaining the integrity of the ring.

campus backbone subsystem: The cabling and crossconnects between clusters of buildings within a site. One building contains the main crossconnect.

carrier sense multiple access with collision detection: The channel access method used by Ethernet and ISO 8802-3 LANs. Each station waits for an idle channel before transmitting and detects overlapping transmissions by other stations.

CCITT (Comite Consultatif International Telegraphique et Telephonique): *See* International Telegraph and Telephone Consultative Committee

CFM: *See* configuration management

claim process: The procedure by which the ring is initialized. It includes negotiation of the target token rotation time and creation of the token.

CMIP: See Common Management Information Protocol

CMT: *See* connection management

code bit: The smallest signaling element used by the Physical layer for transmission on the medium.

code group: The specific sequence of five code bits representing an FDDI symbol.

Common Management Information Protocol: ISO protocol used to exchange system and network management information.

concentrator: An FDDI station that provides attachment points (through M ports) for connecting stations to the FDDI ring. The concentrator is the basic building block of the dual ring of trees topology.

configuration management: That portion of connection management that provides for the configuration of PHY and MAC entities within a station.

configuration switch: The element of SMT that controls the connection of MACs and PHYs in stations and concentrators.

connection management: That portion of the station management function that controls insertion, removal, and connection of the PHY and MAC entities within a station. It includes the physical connection management, configuration management, and entity coordination management components.

controller: A device (single attachment or dual attachment) used to connect end-user stations to the FDDI network; each contains an interface to a specific type of workstation or system.

counter-rotating ring: An arrangement where two signal paths, whose direction of transmission is opposite to each other, exist in a ring topology.

crossconnect: Patch cable and passive hardware that is used to administer the connection of cables at a central or remote location.

CSMA/CD: *See* carrier sense multiple access with collision detection.

DAC: *See* dual attachment concentrator

daemons: A UNIX/ULTRIX term used to describe a background process.

DAS: *See* dual attachment station

Data Link layer: Layer 2 of the OSI model that defines frame construction, addressing, error detection, and other services to higher layers.

decode: The process of recovering the original information from an encoded signal.

decibel: A mathematical expression used to compare the power of two signals.

destination address filtering: A feature of bridges where only frames intended for stations on the extended LAN are forwarded.

doped: The addition of very small amounts of elements to control refractive index.

downstream: A term that refers to the relative position of two stations in a ring. A station is downstream of its neighbor if it receives the token after its neighbor receives the token.

dual attachment concentrator: A concentrator that offers two connections to the FDDI network capable of accommodating the FDDI dual (counter-rotating) ring, and additional ports for connection of other concentrators or FDDI stations.

dual attachment station: An FDDI station that offers two connections to the FDDI dual counter-rotating ring.

dual homing: A method of cabling concentrators and stations in a tree configuration that permits an alternate or backup path to the FDDI network in case the primary connection fails. Can be used in a tree or dual ring of trees configuration.

dual ring of trees: A topology of concentrators and stations that cascade from concentrators on a dual ring.

ECM: *See* entity coordination management

EIA: *See* Electronic Industries Association

elasticity buffer: The function of the PHY standard that deals with the control of clock tolerance between stations. The elasticity buffer guarantees that frames are not lost due to overflow or underflow caused by clock frequency differences between stations.

Electronic Industries Association: A standards organization specializing in the electrical and functional characteristics of interface equipment.

encapsulating bridge: A bridge that forwards frames by enclosing them in an "envelope" that is then removed by another bridge.

encoding: The act of changing data into a series of electrical or optical signals that can travel efficiently over a medium.

entity: An active element within an Open Systems Interconnection layer or sublayer.

entity coordination management: That portion of connection management that provides for controlling bypass relays and signaling to PCM that the medium is available, and for coordinating trace functions.

extended LAN: A collection of LANs interconnected by protocol independent store-and-forward devices (bridges).

FDDI: *See* Fiber Distributed Data Interface

FDDI-II: A 100 Mb/s technology, currently under development in the accredited standards committee, X3T9.5, which supports asynchronous, synchronous, and isochronous services.

Fiber Distributed Data Interface: A set of ANSI/ISO standards that define a high-bandwidth (100 Mb/s) general-purpose LAN. It provides synchronous and asynchronous services between computers and peripheral equipment in a timed-token passing, dual ring of trees configuration.

fiber-optic cable: A transmission medium designed to transmit signals in the form of optical signals.

fiber optics: The technique of using fiber-optic transmitters, receivers, and cables for the transmission of data.

fragment: In FDDI, pieces of a frame left on the ring; caused by a station stripping a frame from the ring.

fragmentation: A process in which large frames from one network are broken up into smaller frames that are compatible with the frame size requirements of the network to which they will be forwarded.

frame: A series of concatenated fields that includes the preamble, start frame delimiter, frame control, source address, destination address, information, frame check sequence, end delimiter field, and control indicators.

graded index: A characteristic of fiber-optic cable in which the core refractive index is varied so that it is high at the center and matches the refractive index of the cladding at the core-cladding boundary.

header: Control information attached to the front of an Ethernet frame by an encapsulating bridge. The header, in conjunction with the trailer, surround the frame prior to the bridge forwarding it to an FDDI network.

hexadecimal: The Base 16 numbering system.

IC: *See* intermediate crossconnect

IEEE: *See* Institute of Electrical and Electronics Engineers

IETF: See Internet Engineering Task Force

index profile: The refractive index of a fiber-optic cable as a function of its distance from the core center.

Institute of Electrical and Electronics Engineers: A professional society of electrical engineers. As part of its various functions, it coordinates, develops, and publishes network standards for use in the United States, following ANSI rules.

interconnect: A panel-mounted fiber-optic coupler or wallbox-mounted fiber-optic coupler used to join two cables with a single pair of connectors.

intermediate crossconnect: An element in the EIA/TIA 568 Commercial Building Wiring standard. Consists of the active, passive, and support components that connect the interbuilding cabling and the intrabuilding cabling for a building.

intermediate system: An OSI term for a system that forwards traffic, and that also originates and terminates traffic. Also referred to as IS.

International Organization for Standardization: An international agency that is responsible for developing, among other things, international standards for information exchange.

International Telegraph and Telephone Consultative Committee:
An international consultative committee that sets international telecommunications and data communications standards.

Internet Engineering Task Force: A task force of the Internet Activi-
ties Board (IAB). The IAB is responsible for the ongoing development
of the Internet. The IETF's responsibilities include specification of
protocols and recommendation of Internet standards, via the Request
for Comment process.

interoperability: The ability of all system elements to exchange information between single vendor and multivendor equipment. Also
called open communications.

ISO: *See* International Organization for Standardization

isochronous transmission: A data communications service required
when time-dependent data is to be transmitted. It is characterized by its
ability to deliver bandwidth at specific, regular intervals.

LAN: *See* local area network

link-loss budget: The total amount of attenuation that can be introduced before an optical system will fail to work.

link state routing: Describes a class of routing algorithms in which
each node floods its local connectivity information (what destinations
it can reach) and neighboring router information (what routers it is adjacent to) to all nodes in some defined, closed set of routers. This allows
all routers in the closed set to obtain complete topology information
about the routers in the set, and to then run an identical routing algorithm in order to obtain a consistent set of routes.

LLC: *See* Logical Link Control

local area network: A data communications network that spans a limited geographical area. The network provides high-bandwidth communication over coaxial cable, twisted-pair, fiber, or microwave media. It
is usually owned by the user.

Logical Link Control: Part of the Data Link layer of the OSI model. It
defines services for the transmission of data between two stations with
no intermediate switching stations.

logical ring: The path a token follows in an FDDI network made up of all the connected MAC sublayers. The accompanying physical topology can be a dual ring of trees, a tree, or a ring.

logical topology: *See* logical ring

low-cost fiber: A standard (LCF-PMD) under development by X3T9.5 that aims to reduce the cost of fiber optic connections to FDDI stations. The standard will define a link distance of up to 500 meters and use a duplex SC connector as its MIC.

MAC: *See* Media Access Control

MAC-bridge: A term used to describe any Data Link layer bridge.

main crossconnect: An element in the EIA/TIA 568 Commercial Building Wiring standard. Consists of the active, passive, and support components that connect the interbuilding backbone cables to intermediate crossconnects.

Management Information Base: The repository of manageable attributes of a managed system. The FDDI MIB specifies the components of a station that can be managed.

MAU: See Multistation Access Unit

MC: *See* main crossconnect

Media Access Control: The Data Link sublayer responsible for scheduling, transmitting, and receiving data on a shared medium LAN (for example, FDDI).

media interface connector: An optical fiber connector pair that links the fiber media to the FDDI station or another cable. The MIC consists of two halves. The MIC plug terminates an optical fiber cable. The MIC receptacle is attached to an FDDI station.

MIB: See Management Information Base

MIC: *See* media interface connector

multimode: A type of fiber optic cable in which more than one transmission mode is supported.

Multistation Access Unit: The device that attaches token ring stations to an 802.5 ring.

Network layer: Layer 3 of the OSI model that is responsible for network-wide addressing, and routing of frames between networks.

node: Any device connected to a network (for example, workstation, concentrator, bridge).

nonreturn to zero: A data transmission technique in which a logical level, high or low, represents a logical 1 or 0.

nonreturn to zero invert on ones: A data transmission technique in which a polarity transition from low to high, or high to low, represents a logical 1. No polarity transition represents a logical 0.

NRZ: *See* nonreturn to zero

NRZI: *See* nonreturn to zero invert on ones

Open Systems Interconnection: Internationally accepted framework of standards for intersystem communication. It is modeled by a seven layer model, developed by the International Organization for Standardization, which covers all aspects of information exchange between two systems.

OSI: *See* Open Systems Interconnection

PCM: *See* physical connection management

peer-to-peer: Assigning of communications tasks so that data transmission between logical groups or layers in a network architecture is accomplished between entities in the same sublayer of the OSI model.

PHY: *See* Physical Layer Protocol

physical connection: In FDDI, the full-duplex physical layer association between adjacent PHYs.

physical connection management: That portion of connection management that manages the physical connect between adjacent PHYs. This includes the signaling of connection type, link confidence testing, and the enforcement of connection rules.

Physical layer: Layer 1 of the OSI model that defines and handles the electrical and physical connections between systems. The physical layer can also encode data into a form that is compatible with the medium.

Physical Layer Medium Dependent: FDDI standards that define the media and protocols to transfer symbols between adjacent PHYs.

Physical Layer Protocol: FDDI standard that defines symbols, line states, clocking requirements, and the encoding of data for transmission.

physical topology: The actual arrangement of cables and hardware that make up the network.

PMD: *See* Physical Layer Medium Dependent

power budget: The difference between transmit power and receiver sensitivity, including any tolerances.

power penalty: The total loss introduced by planned-for splices in the fiber link. Typically, extra splices are planned but not immediately implemented.

preamble: A sequence of idle symbols transmitted before each frame. Its purpose is to aid in clock synchronization of the receiving station.

propagation delay: The time it takes for a signal to travel across the network.

protocol filtering: A feature in which some bridges can be programmed to always forward or always reject frames that are originated under specified protocols.

protocols: Set of operating rules and procedures governing peer-to-peer communications over a network.

refractive index: The ratio of the speed of light in a material, relative to the speed of light in a vacuum.

repeat: The process by which a station receives a frame or token from its upstream neighbor, retimes it, and transmits it to its downstream neighbor. The repeating station can examine, copy to a buffer, and/or modify control bits in the frame as appropriate.

repeater: A level 1 hardware device that performs the basic actions of restoring signal amplitude and timing of signals before transmission onto another network segment.

ring: Connection of two or more stations in a circular logical topology. Information is passed sequentially between active stations, each one in turn examining or copying the data, and finally returning it to the originating station, which removes it from the network.

ring management: The portion of SMT responsible for detection and resolution of duplicate address and stuck beacon conditions.

RIP: See Routing Information Protocol.

router: A level 3 hardware device that uses layer 3 protocols to forward frames to end-stations or other routers.

Routing Information Protocol: An example of a distance vector routing protocol that has been used for routing of IP, IPX, and XNS protocols.

SAC: *See* single attachment concentrator

SAS: *See* single attachment station

sensitivity: The minimum power required for proper reception of a signal by an optical receiver.

shielded twisted pair: A twisted pair cable whose resistance to electromagnetic interference is improved by use of a flexible metallic sheath surrounding the pairs. In the context of FDDI, it usually refers to 150-Ohm cables such as Type 1 cable.

ships-in-the-night: Refers to routing algorithms that operate independently of each other.

Simple Network Management Protocol: Application layer, standards-based protocol for network management, used in TCP/IP networks.

single attachment concentrator: A concentrator that offers one S port for attachment to the FDDI network, and M ports for the attachment of stations or other concentrators.

single attachment station: An FDDI station that offers one S port for attachment to the FDDI ring.

single mode: A type of fiber optic cable in which only one transmission mode is supported.

SMT: *See* Station Management

SNMP: *See* Simple Network Management Protocol

source address filtering: A feature of some bridges where frames from designated source addresses are either always forwarded or always rejected.

spanning tree: A method of creating a loop-free logical topology on an extended LAN. Formation of a spanning tree topology for transmission of frames across bridges is based on the industry-standard spanning tree algorithm defined in IEEE 802.1d.

station: A node on an FDDI ring capable of transmitting, receiving, and repeating data. A station has one instance of SMT, at least one instance of PHY and PMD, and an optional MAC entity.

Station Management: The entity within a station on the FDDI ring that monitors station activity and exercises overall control of station activity. Also refers to the SMT standard under development by ANSI X3T9.5.

step index: A characteristic of fiber-optic cable in which the refractive index of the core material is uniform. A sudden change (or step) of the refractive index exists at the core-cladding boundary.

stripping: The process by which a station removes its transmitted frames from the ring.

stuck beacon: The condition where a station continuously sends beacon frames.

symbol: The smallest signaling element used by FDDI. The symbol set consists of sixteen data symbols and sixteen non-data symbols. Each symbol corresponds to a specific sequence of code bits (code group) to be transmitted by the Physical layer.

synchronous transmission: An FDDI service class which guarantees a certain bandwidth to each requesting station, within a time bounded by the timed-token protocol.

target token rotation time: The value used by the MAC sublayer to time its operations. The TTRT value varies, depending on the operational state of the ring.

TC: *See* telecommunications closet

telecommunications closet: An element in the EIA/TIA 568 Commercial Building Wiring standard. The location for crossconnects and active, passive, and support components that provide the connection between the building backbone cabling and the horizontal wiring.

Telecommunications Industries Association: TIA was formed from the Electronic Industries Association (EIA) and the United States Telecommunications Buyers Association. The TIA fiber-optic committees develop and publish testing standards and specifications for fiber-optic components and systems.

ThinWire: A small diameter (50-ohm) coaxial cable used in 802.3 and FDDI networks.

TIA: *See* Telecommunications Industries Association

timed-token protocol: The rules defining how the target token rotation time is set, the length of time a station can hold the token, and how the ring is initialized.

token: A bit pattern consisting of a unique symbol sequence that circulates around the ring following frame transmission. The token grants stations the right to transmit.

token holding timer: A timer that controls the amount of time a station may hold the token in order to transmit asynchronous frames.

token passing: A method where each station, in turn, receives and passes on the right to use the channel. In FDDI, the stations are configured in a logical ring.

token rotation timer: A timer that times the period between the receipt of tokens.

trace: A diagnostic process to recover from a stuck-beacon condition. The trace operation localizes a fault to the beaconing MAC and its upstream neighbor MAC.

trailer: *See* header

translating bridge: A nonproprietary MAC layer device used to connect similar and dissimilar LANs according to 802.1d, 802.1h, and 802.1i rules.

TRT: *See* token rotation timer

TTRT: *See* target token rotation time

TVX: *See* valid transmission timer

twisted pair: A communications cable constructed of two helically wrapped conductors.

unshielded twisted pair: A cable constructed of two helically wrapped conductors that are called a pair. In the context of FDDI, it usually refers to 100-Ohm cables in a 4-pair bundle.

upstream: A term that refers to the relative position of two stations in a ring. A station is upstream of its neighbor if it receives the token before its neighbor receives the token.

valid transmission timer: A timer that times the period between valid transmissions on the ring; used to detect excessive ring noise, token loss, and other faults.

WAN: *See* wide area network

wide area network: A network spanning a large geographical area that provides communications among devices on a regional, national, or international basis.

window: As relates to a fiber-optic cable, a window refers to a wavelength region of relatively high transmittance, surrounded by regions of low transmittance.

workgroup: A network configuration characterized by a small number of attached devices spread over a limited geographical area.

Index